Confessions

of a

Demonized Christian

How I received another "Jesus," then overcame the imposters

DAVID HADDON

CHESED BOOKS
REDDING, CALIFORNIA

To the glory of God
with thanksgiving for my mother,
Vera Parks Haddon,
who loved me deeply and early schooled me in the Scriptures

Contents

Acknowledgements

I am indebted to all of the authors listed in the bibliography, especially to those mentioned in the text. Two of these stand out, the late G. W. Exel and the late Ron Dunn. Mr. Exel's crucial part in my story is described in Chapter 13. And Ron was my pastor at MacArthur Boulevard Baptist Church in Irving, Texas, during my ordeal. His discovering, living and preaching the lordship of Jesus Christ were a great encouragement to me.

A respected deliverance minister was kind enough to read and helpfully critique my manuscript. He pointed out to me, among other things, that hatred and confusion are leading indicators of demonization that I had neglected to mention as such. While we agreed on the basic thesis of this book that a Christian can be demonized and on many other aspects, our differences on some matters were such that acknowledgement by name might associate him with positions he doesn't share. But I do thank him for those of his suggestions that I adopted, significantly improving my text.

I thank Dr. Jack Painter, who teaches New Testament Greek at Simpson University in Redding, California, for his criticisms of Chapter 20, which helped me sharpen my argument precisely because of our differences.

And although I have read *The Lord of the Rings* three times, I must credit a 2001 essay by Gene Edward Veith ("Still Ringing True," *World Magazine*) with calling to my attention Aragorn's words from *The Two Towers* that I used as the epigraph for Chapter 10. This passage may be one of those in the trilogy that C. S. Lewis said expressed "beauties which pierce like swords or burn like cold iron." I was struck by this gust of the fresh winds of a transcendent morality blowing over the grassy plains of Rohan. Thus art reveals the beauties of holiness.

I thank Mark Buschgens of Marked by Design in Redding for translating my concept for the covers of this book into reality.

I thank Shirley for her accurate work in typing up my handwritten journal now these many years ago.

Responsibility for any errors of observation or of exposition of demonology or of God's gracious provision for our deliverance from the devil is entirely my own.

"'For I know the plans I have for you,' declares the Lord 'plans for wholeness and not for evil, to give you a future and a hope'" (Jeremiah 29:11, ESV).

Introduction

Many authors have written of affliction by demons, but my *Confessions of a Demonized Christian* is unusual in being a frank, first-person account of how—although I was already a Christian—my own sins and a demonic lie led first to my occupation and then to my affliction by demons.

I have written these confessions to help Christians afflicted by demons understand both the causes of their affliction and how their identity in Christ gives them authority over those demons. Then my personal story of how—by God's grace—I overcame my demons gives an example for applying the biblical principles of the Christian's identity and authority in Christ. In addition, by exposing the demons' methods of operation, I want to help other at-risk Christians avoid invasion by demons entirely.

Christian Writer Since 1973

My track record as a Christian writer since 1973 is one of seriousness of purpose and the absence of sensationalism. And *all* my Christian writing was done *after* having been demonized in 1970. My first major Christian publication was my exposé in *Christianity Today* (December 21, 1973) of Maharishi Mahesh Yogi's deceptive presentation of Transcendental Meditation (TM) as non-religious to insinuate it into American public schools. That was followed by InterVarsity Press's booklet on TM (1974) and by *TM Wants You!* (Baker, 1976), which I co-authored with Vail Hamilton (Carruth), a former teacher of TM.

My degrees are a BS in Engineering from UC Berkeley and an interdisciplinary MA in Politics and Literature from the University of Dallas. With this academic background, I have published articles on subjects ranging from quantum mechanics (*Touchstone,*

September 2003) to the rescue of Jews in Le Chambon, France. In addition, I have critiqued some of the Harry Potter books for *American Spectator Online* and the pro-life journal, *Celebrate Life.* My most recent essay, on the surprising morality of Jack London's "To Build a Fire," appeared in *Touchstone,* January/February 2012.

Demonization Defined

The New Testament Greek word "demonize" (*daimonizomai*) denotes being under the power of a demon or demons. I suffered demonization as a pervasive occupation of my body and a devastating affliction of my soul by demons, in which they subjected me to agonies of fear and anxiety and various physical afflictions. Forms of this Greek verb are usually translated as "demon-possessed," but the demons never succeeded in suppressing my mind and gaining complete control of my body. For this and other reasons given in Chapter 20, I prefer to use "demonized," the corresponding English form of the Greek verb, to describe any demon occupation of a human being.

Although not demonized to the point of complete demon control, I did have one Hell of a fight because my body was already thoroughly occupied by evil spirits before I realized that they were demons. Nevertheless, despite their determined efforts to destroy me, God's grace was sufficient. And what I learned through my experience in using the Scriptures and other means of grace against them will be helpful to any demonized Christian.

I received these demons at first gradually and imperceptibly through habitual sexual sin and later rapidly and palpably through false mystical experiences. But there are many other avenues to demonization of believers because sins such as hatred, unforgiveness, occultism, and drug use have the same temporal consequences for Christians as for Pagans: demonization. This to-some unpalatable reality has been recognized by many Christian scholars and leaders including Dr. Neil T. Anderson, Dr. Keith M. Bailey, Dr. Mark I. Bubeck, Dr. C. Fred Dickason, Dr. Ed Murphy and the late Dr. Merrill F. Unger. I share their view of this controverted subject not only from my experience, but also on the basis of the Scriptures. (See Chapter 20. Bible Evidence that a Christian Can Have a Demon, p. 109 ff.)

Why Such Frank Confessions?

The purpose and form of my *Confessions* require me to reveal the sins that allowed demons to come into my body. This is humbling, and I would not do it publicly were it not necessary to make clear how sexual sin makes us vulnerable to entry by demons. In addition, to show exactly how demons entered my life requires that I expose the sins of other family members now dead, something that filial piety would forbid were it not for the importance of this material in enabling readers to understand 1) How the devil operates in families and 2) How our sins can harm others in our families.

I don't dwell on my sins more than necessary, but my mention of them may yet disturb those for whom the "M-word" is taboo. Indeed, one pastor suggested to me that perhaps the reason the publishers I contacted did not publish my manuscript was my frank discussion of masturbation (as sin). If that is true, perhaps one reason that alarming numbers of Christian men and even pastors are said to remain addicted to pornography is that they are unwilling to confess their sin of lust under the humiliating name of the activity for the enhancement of which they pay good money to pornographers. Perhaps they are not desperate enough to admit just what they use their pornography for. But the most crucial reason for continuing addictions among Christians may be that they have not recognized and gotten rid of the demons they picked up through their sins and that continue to bind them to their sinful addictions.

Help and Hope for the Demonized

Because habitual sexual sin gives place to the devil just as much as do hatred, unforgiveness, occultism, and drug use; this book will be helpful to those addicted to pornography as well as to those with other addictions. Since overcoming any of these sinful practices may require exercising the authority of the name of Jesus against the demons involved, recognition of their presence may be the missing link necessary for complete and permanent victory over such addictions.

And there is certainly hope in Christ for all such habitual sinners and addicts, just as there is for other demonized Christians. So this book is addressed to all Christians afflicted by the devil as well as to those called to minister to them. For the cautionary yet hopeful story of how I became demonized and then, by the power of God's word, by the blood of the Lamb and by the word of my testimony that Jesus Christ is Lord, was restored to effective service in Christ's kingdom; read the book.

Freedom from Fear and Anxiety

But if reading this Introduction has caused you any fear or anxiety, be sure that this book was written especially for you. For my book will show you how, as a believer, your exalted identity in Christ, your authority in his exalted name and the power of God's holy word can free you from fear and anxiety for life.

David Haddon
July 2012
Redding, California

Part 1: Hidden Warfare

"Save me, O God! For the waters have come up to my neck"
(Psalm 69:1, ESV).

1

Hitting the Wall

"**I**'ve got to get out of here!" is the idea that takes hold of me, as I unwillingly get up from my desk. As a graduate student facing finals, I have stacks of reading to do and nothing in my cozy dorm room is amiss. But an overwhelming restlessness drives me out the door of my room and into the dimly lit corridor. As I turn to the right and begin to walk down the vinyl-tiled hall towards the light red double doors leading outside to the darkness of the December night, fear wells up within me for no apparent reason.

On the inside I feel as if I were filled up to the neck with water, as if I were about to drown. Then, the thought strikes me, "Have I been possessed by demons?" And this question adds a surge of panic to the anxiety and fear already gripping me.

It was a Saturday evening, December 12, 1970, and I'd been sitting alone at my desk in my single room. I was the only graduate student in the modest, two-story men's dormitory at the small Texas University where I had been for three semesters. As a Vietnam-era veteran who had volunteered for Special Forces duty in 1963, my expenses were well covered by my GI Bill benefits and a full scholarship in the school's interdisciplinary program in Politics and Literature. Indeed, in the previous year my disciplined study habits had helped make me a leading student in my first-year class in the 3-year graduate program. But now, my iron discipline had cracked, and I abandoned my futile effort to study. The reality that no one can serve two masters was being played out in my body and soul as both God and the devil asserted their conflicting claims on me.

Return to the Faith

Only 7 months before, after about 17 years of backsliding, at 31 years of age, I had returned to faith in Jesus Christ. My whole world was brightened by my experience of God's forgiveness and the love and joy it brought. My ingrained habit of masturbation that had broken my fellowship with the Lord many years earlier just fell away. And I immediately began to share my faith with others, for whom I had a new spiritual concern. In Jesus Christ, I had rediscovered the meaning of life.

When I returned to the college in the fall for the second year of course work in the doctoral program, I continued to excel in my studies. Better yet, in the nearby town, I had discovered a Southern Baptist Church where the Spirit of revival was overflowing in praise, prayer and powerful preaching. With such sweet fellowship in the Holy Spirit so near, it seemed that nothing could harm me.

Doing Things Right?

Yet now in December, I found myself gripped by inner terrors like nothing I had ever known. That isn't how it was supposed to work! Silently I cried out to God for help, but he seemed distant, not like the physically palpable spiritual presences I had come to accept in the delightful spiritual experiences I had been having since shortly after coming back to the Lord.

During the summer, I had appropriated Psalm 63 as an apt description of my special spiritual experiences: "O God, you are my God, earnestly I seek you; my soul thirsts for you, *my body* longs for you . . . . *On my bed* I remember you" (vv. 1a, 6a). As if in confirmation, on a Sunday while driving back to Texas from California, I attended a church in Santa Barbara where the sermon text was from Psalm 63. I took this as a sign from God that my self-serving interpretation of the Psalm was right. The Scriptures do sometimes use physical imagery to describe the soul's relationship with God, but I had misused such passages to justify the sensuous basis of my false spiritual experiences.

After all, I had thought, didn't my special spiritual experiences bolster my faith in the reality of the invisible God in the midst of a skeptical world? Hadn't God given me victory over my sins of lust and masturbation? Didn't I understand the Bible as never before? And wasn't I in fellowship at a solid church in the midst of a spiritual revival based on making Jesus Christ Lord of our lives?

Because I could see real spiritual progress going along with my special spiritual experiences, I thought that they, too, must be of God. It's true that about 6 weeks earlier I had had some real doubts about those experiences. An inward physical pressure within my nose that I associated with the spiritual presences had become so painfully intense on Halloween, ominously enough, that I decided to stop receiving them. But the experiences were usually so pleasant that I had not persisted in rejecting them and their underlying evil spirits—for that is what they were.

And now I was suddenly in such anguish and terror that I feared falling under demonic control, becoming violent and being put into a mental ward. I feared being permanently left at the mercy of unbelieving psychiatrists who could not understand, let alone treat, such a condition of demon possession.

The Struggle to Survive

In an agony of fear, I continue walking down that vinyl-tiled hallway and out through the red double doors to the parking lot near the dorm. There my familiar, two-toned light and dark blue 1956 Chevy hardtop is parked, invitingly. I think of going for a drive to relax and relieve my distress, but I don't dare risk it because I'm not sure I can control myself and drive safely. And I don't know anyone at the college to whom I can go for immediate help with such a grave spiritual problem. Sooner or later I return to my dorm room, but I can't remember much of what happened or how I got through that terrible night. I was caught in the middle: Satan couldn't make me do anything against my will, and God was waiting for the demonic emotional torment to help me to realize my sin and repent from it.

My confusion was great, and my fear seemed ready to explode into uncontrollable panic. For an entire week, I struggled not to freak out while I somehow completed my finals. At the campus library, the distress on my face was so obvious that a kindly Cistercian monk from the nearby monastery asked me what was wrong. I don't remember what I told him, but he gave me a Scripture about suffering for the name of Christ from 1 Peter 4. Although I still didn't realize what had happened to me, I didn't see myself as suffering for Christ and found no comfort in that or any other Scripture. Indeed, perhaps the most damaging effect of my misuse of Psalm 63 was that, when I realized what I had done, I overreacted against my misuse of that psalm and Psalms became a closed book to me just when I most needed their comfort and encouragement.

Overcoming the Fear of Demons

Deceived as I was, it still seemed to me that I had been doing everything right. My genuine spiritual progress blinded me to the unpalatable reality that, shortly after my return to faith, I had been seduced by a deceiving spirit, by a demon. The results were devastating for a time, but as costly as my spiritual adultery has been to me, I believe that my sins, like those of the Israelites, are valuable as "examples and were written down as warnings for us on whom the fulfillment of the ages has come" (1 Corinthians 10:11). Indeed, if reading of my encounter with demons has caused you any fear, my story has been written especially for you. Reading my whole story will help you to face and overcome your fears through a biblical approach to unleashing the Christian's inheritance of the authority of the name of the Lord Jesus Christ and of the power of his word, the Bible.

So how had I so quickly fallen into a demonic pit while earnestly seeking—and, indeed, finding—God? To answer this and other questions about how seducing spirits work, I must tell you what had happened to me in my youth that left me so vulnerable to demonic seduction when I returned to Jesus as my Lord. Let's begin at my beginning in a little coal company town on the west side of the Colorado Rockies in the next chapter, "A Divided Spiritual Heritage."

"I will put enmity between you and the woman, and between your offspring and her offspring" (Genesis 3:15, ESV).

2

A Divided Spiritual Heritage

In June 1938, I was born, the youngest son of Earl and Vera Haddon, in Mount Harris, Colorado, a coal-company town that no longer exists. America was still in the shadow of the Great Depression, but Dad had found work in a soft coal mine on the west side of the Rocky Mountains between Steamboat Springs and Craig, Colorado. There my father labored hard in the Victor-American Mine to support the family.

"And Deeper in Debt"

So my beginnings are bound up with my father's work in the dark and dangerous depths of that mine, where he broke his leg in an accident. He recovered, but his being off work while his leg healed left the family deeply in debt to the mining company because Mount Harris was a company town. The mining company owned almost everything, the mine, the bathhouse, the houses, the store and the hotel. By the time Dad was able to go back to work, the family owed the company about $600 for rent and groceries, big money in those days. So the Haddon family could relate to the indebtedness Tennessee Ernie Ford later sang about in his 1950s hit "Sixteen Tons" (by Merle Travis). After recounting the miner's hard labor loading 16 tons of coal, the song's chorus concludes with the miner's regretful command to Saint Peter not to call him since he can't go to Heaven because he owes his soul to the company store.

Dad was called "Shorty" by his friends on the job because he was only about 5 feet 3 inches tall. But he had the bulging muscles of the working man to show for his labor. He rejected both God and Capitalism, holding to Anarchism and to Marxist ideas of class struggle. He sometimes sang "Solidarity Forever" from the songbook of the International Workers of the World (Wobblies). And I suspect that the dark history of the Colorado mining companies' bloody suppression of miners' strikes using hired gunmen and even the Colorado National Guard contributed to his distrust of the American system of economics and government. Since Mom didn't go along with his Marxist ideas, we didn't hear much about them at home except when Dad would sing the songs from his Wobbly song book along with some Stephen Foster songs like "My Old Kentucky Home."

Bogeymen, No! Bible, Yes!

Mom worked hard at home taking care of her husband and four boys. She was adamantly against the superstitions that had been pressed upon her by adults in the Texas of her childhood. She particularly resented the stories of bogeymen used to frighten her and other children into "being good" and never spoke of them except to debunk them. Mom scorned the bad luck of Friday the 13th, broken mirrors and walking under ladders. Any talk of ghosts brought a firm, "There's no such thing as ghosts." Mom's healthy skepticism of old superstitions didn't stop her from believing everything the Bible said including all its miracles and the existence of God, angels, demons and the devil, as well as of a Hell to be shunned and a Heaven to be gained.

In its striking contradiction of my mother's skepticism about ghosts, one early childhood nightmare stands out in my mind. In the dream, I am looking at the back of a derelict car of 1930s vintage in the dark of night. Someone says, "That car is haunted." Confident in the truth of my mother's denial of ghosts and determined to disprove this contrary claim, I boldly say, "Ghost, come out!" Instantly, to my great surprise and utter horror, out of the absent rear window's opening a menacing spirit floats, looking like a giant white caterpillar with a hateful yellow face on the front end. I don't remember whether it spoke or not, but I awoke in terror and still remember the dream, although it never recurred. Despite that memorable nightmare, I didn't believe in ghosts, but I was afraid of the dark and of scary stories of the supernatural. So perhaps a seed of fear was sown in me by that strange dream.

I Remember Pearl Harbor: December 7, 1941

In the summer of 1941 when I was 3, and despite the $600 we owed to the mining company; we left Mount Harris and moved to California. We had enough money to do this because the miners' union had forced the mine owners to pay the miners in cash instead of in company scrip, the situation that led to the debt slavery referred to in "Sixteen Tons." Dad left first to find work near Sacramento, where my dad's brother, Clyde Haddon, lived. Later Mom followed him with us kids.

Of course I was unaware of it, but since 1939, besides the lingering Depression, America had been living under another shadow, that of the War in Europe. The explosion of that war into American territory in the Pacific when Japan attacked Pearl Harbor, Hawaii, on December 7, 1941, is another of my earliest memories. That Sunday afternoon, Mom and I were at church where she was helping with a rehearsal of the Sunday school Christmas program. Someone brought the news of the Japanese attack, the rehearsal ended abruptly and we all went home. My three brothers met us outside of the house we had rented with further news of the attack. Although I was only three years old, I realized that something huge had happened because my mom and brothers were so struck by the news, and I still remember that day.

Early in 1942, we heard more bad news, this time from Colorado. On January 27, an explosion in the Victor-American Mine, where my Dad had worked before we left, had killed 34 miners. Dad knew all of these men because the blast occurred on his shift. Our flight from Colorado had been most timely.

Childhood Traumas

In the basement of the house we rented in New Castle, there was a small storage cupboard that I could just fit into. For some inexplicable reason, I thought it would be fun to have my brothers shut me up in that little space. In mother's absence, they readily agreed to my idea, but as soon as they shut the door on me and it got dark, I panicked and screamed for them to let me out. Remarkably, they quickly opened the door. Had they been less compassionate, I think that I could have suffered a more severe trauma. As it was, I suffered only a slight tendency to claustrophobia, which has largely dissipated. According to those experienced in ministry to the demon afflicted, children subjected to extreme danger and fear can receive demons as a result. I don't think this experience was severe enough to open a door to demons in my life, but another seed of fear was sown in me, and demons would later use my fearfulness to isolate me from those who could have helped me resist their influence.

Media and Morality

Mom understood the GIGO (garbage in/garbage out) principle in selecting children's comic books long before we ever heard of TV, let alone computers. Therefore, violent comic book superheroes (even Superman) were out. But as compensation, I had my very own subscription to Walt Disney's Donald Duck. When it arrived by mail every month she usually would read it to me before my brothers got to see it. I still remember in detail one strongly moral episode from the Disney comics of that era

At Bechtel Camp in the woods of Northern California near the Big Bend of the Pitt River where Dad worked on a hydroelectric dam project, I had a couple of practical moral lessons about anger and violence. Although I was a compliant child, Mom's intuition that she should limit my exposure to comic book violence was well founded. When crossed, I attacked others. Once, I hit a playmate with a stick when he did something I didn't like. And when my brother Leonard seized my toy gun and shot me in the face with its harmless, rubber-tipped dart, I slashed him with my penknife. He bears the scar of my mayhem on his shoulder to this day. Fortunately, my violent attacks were met with rebukes: my playmate hit me back and my mother took my penknife away.

These rebukes discouraged me from using violence to vent my anger or get my way and may have inclined me to timidity. On the other hand, had my violent impulses in these early encounters been unchecked, I could easily have become a bully. These wouldn't be my last resorts to violence, but I did learn to prefer other means to get my way. Providentially, my mother knew what I really needed to put me on the right path and would soon begin to give it to me in healthy doses.

"How can a young man cleanse his way? By taking heed according to Your word" (Psalm 119:9, NKJV).

3

Thy Word Is a Lamp unto My Feet

In 1943 we moved to Redding, then a town of about 8,000 at the north end of California's Sacramento Valley. Dad worked as a rock driller on nearby Shasta Dam. Having returned from the wilderness to town, Mom insisted that the family settle down in Redding so my three older brothers could complete high school there. Perhaps because he knew by painful experience of the need for that high school diploma, Dad acquiesced despite what Mom called his "itchy foot."

The Little Brown Shingle House on West Street

In Redding, we first lived at 1320 West Street in a small, darkly weathered shingle house approached by a wooden bridge across an open concrete-lined storm drain called Calaboose Creek.

For a family of six, the house was tiny. Two of my brothers had bunk beds and I had a little trundle bed that was slid under my parents' double bed during the day. When Dad was home, we were quiet at night so he could get his sleep for his next hard day's work. But when he worked a night shift, we were all in earshot of each other and had some memorable family conversations during one of which Mom revealed to me that there wasn't a Santa Claus so that I wouldn't be teased about it when I started school.

We shared a back yard of sorts with other tenants, and a little black kitten appeared there. So I petted it until it purred and then followed my natural impulse and dropped it into some shallow water in the open storm drain. Seeing the defenseless kitten's utter revulsion from and fear of the water gave me a visceral thrill like nothing else I had ever done. So I set about to regain the kitten's confidence and with some difficulty did so. Then, of course, I did it again! From this second betrayal, however, the kitten learned that I could not be trusted and it never came near me again. The poor kitten's pathetic dismay, fright and permanent flight from me finally touched my conscience. My cruelty to that kitten pained me for years afterwards and moderated my budding sadism. I never told Mom what I had done to the kitten, but she knew what I needed anyway.

Line upon Line

Well before I started first grade, my mother and I together learned by heart Psalm 1 and John 1:1-5. I still recite Psalm 1 in the King James Version in which we learned it, but I have relearned the passage from John in a modern version and extended it to include the entire Prologue. We stopped at verse 5 in John's gospel because the subject shifted there from Christ to John the Baptist, whom Mom considered much less interesting. Of course, she also taught me the usual passages like John 3:16, the Lord's Prayer, the Twenty Third Psalm and Psalm 100. But Psalm 1 and John 1:1-5 are special to me because she didn't teach them to me; we both learned them together.

The Big Yellow House on Eureka Way

During WW-II housing was hard to find for a family with four children, but my smart Mom found a house with five rooms and bath only two blocks away at 1949 Eureka Way for a "reasonable" $20 a month. It sat on a hill high above the street. Tall, old-fashioned windows and 12-foot ceilings gave the five-room house a light and airy atmosphere in contrast with the tiny, dark place where we had been living.

Not content with our having memorized some Scriptures, Mom started home schooling me in the Bible even before I started first grade and learned to read. She used Roper's 12-booklet, 3-year *Through the Bible Study for Children*. At first Mom would ask me the questions, read me the Scriptures with the answer, and then write down my oral replies in the booklet. I still have those little yellow workbooks, which show my progress from printing out a few answers in the first book to writing most of the shorter answers in the last book.

School Days Begin

Not long after we moved into the big yellow house, I had to begin school. Despite my mother's wise preparations, I was still anxious about school and that first day was rough. For some reason, I got into a fight with another boy even before the first bell had rung, ending our wrestling match. Then, at the first recess, I was greeted by a harsh, "Get out of here!" by the girls into whose bathroom I had innocently strayed.

My first grade teacher, Mrs. H., was strong on discipline and detail. But my anxieties about school were short lived because I excelled in reading.

Billy and Me

Billy became my closest playmate because he lived next door. Because Mom took me to Sunday school and church, I knew that a Christian was supposed to tell others about God. But I didn't understand the gospel and hadn't yet been converted myself. Having become a conscientious boy, I urged faith in God upon Billy. When he said he believed in God, I thought that he must be saved and told him so. My rush to assure him of salvation was premature, of course. Happily, we spent most of the time playing cowboys and Indians on stick horses with Billy's imagination providing the plot line for our adventures..

But our friendship had some rocky times, too. One day when he and his older brother were at my house, he kept squirting me with a water gun until I got so mad that I started a fistfight with him. But suddenly, my sensitive conscience kicked in and I realized that I had sinned. Without a word, I abruptly stopped fighting and sat down in a chair. He continued to pummel me until his brother restrained him. My brother, not understanding my conduct, was embarrassed by my apparent cowardice and rebuked me sharply for it after they left. And I didn't even try to explain to him my sudden attack of scruples.

The incident left me feeling that I was a coward and wondering about how to obey Jesus' command to turn the other cheek. Like most children after a quarrel, Billy and I continued to play our games with hardly a thought about it. But I felt I had lost the respect of my brother for a long time. The powerful way my ideas about God affected my conduct seemed like a curse at the time, but now I see how much more dangerous it is for people to profess a faith in God that has no effect on their conduct.

A Child's Fascination with Magical Power

Outdoor play came to an abrupt halt at 5:00 pm when the 15-minute adventure programs like Tom Mix and his Ralston Straight Shooters, Ovaltine's Captain Midnight and Superman came on the air one after the other. Although the stacks of Superman, Batman and Human Torches comic books that Billy had were still off limits for me, my mother did let me listen to all these programs. Donald Duck was still my mainstay in comics, but sometimes Mom would grant my plea for a Super Rabbit comic book. I can still remember what a deep, visceral thrill I got every time the innocuous little rabbit hero said the magic word *"Shazzam"* and with a lightning bolt was transformed into the garishly costumed and mighty Super Rabbit. Not the crime fighting, but the magic it was that turned me on; the magical transformation gave me a mysterious thrill.

The intensity of this thrill was similar to the sadistic thrill I got by mistreating the kitten, but without the bite of wounded conscience afterwards. I think the experience also differed in its mysterious and wonderful sense of participation in magical power. Perhaps because children are small and weak, they are easily intrigued by the prospect of godlike, supernatural power that is the lure of the occult. This prospect was part of the temptation of Adam and Eve and has a continuing attraction for all of their descendents, whatever their age. The Super Rabbit stories, however, had no other occult elements to turn my mind in that direction, so their potential for harm was probably small. The same cannot be said of the immensely popular Harry Potter series with its detailed descriptions of various occult entities, practices and the occult principles of the magician who believes he can change reality by concentrating his attention and focusing his will power on his desired ends.

Super Rabbit/Super Boy

Indeed, an experience like my own intense vicarious yet visceral response to this fictional transformation of a weak, childlike figure into Super Rabbit by the exercise of magical power may be integral to the Harry Potter phenomenon. Harry's transformation into a child wizard exercising power sufficient to stand up to and finally overcome the awesome power of the dark wizard Voldemort parallels the transformation of that puny rabbit into Super Rabbit. Even assuming as I do that this phenomenon is psycho-physiological, when it is joined to the sustained, vicarious initiation into the practice of occultism provided by J. K. Rowling's books, the potential for spiritual mischief is real.

The magician's principles of controlling reality by his *concentration* and *willpower* introduced in the Harry Potter books are dangerous even if young readers merely use them to imitate Harry's fictional spell casting, as they will be tempted to do. The greater danger is that, having been familiarized with the concept of using occult power as a means of doing good, they will seek the real-world sources of occult knowledge and power so readily available on the internet and in most book shops.

Consider the Apostle's loving concern for the Roman Christians when he said, "I want you to be wise about what is good, and innocent about what is evil" (Romans 16:19b). That is what my mother wanted for me. Those parents today who—like my mother—want to protect their children from the Evil One will seek out superior children's literature by authors with worldviews consonant with Christianity instead of J. K Rowling's nominally Christian but actually Neopagan worldview.

Media Today

Television was unseen in Redding until I was a teenager and thus had little influence on my life. But today TV seems always with us except in homes that intentionally banish it. In its threefold challenge to godliness, TV desensitizes the young to violence, unremittingly challenges sexual purity in its advertising as well as in its programming and, perhaps most damning, inculcates a spirit deadening consumerism into adults and children alike.

TV advertising, quite aside from its seductive use of sex to sell everything, constantly teaches the anti-biblical notion that things will fulfill us. In the Temptation, by contrast, Christ quoted Moses who said, "Man shall not live by bread alone, but by every word that comes from the mouth of God" (Matt. 4:4, ESV). Later, in the

Sermon on the Mount, Jesus told us to store up treasures in heaven instead of on earth for, "You cannot serve God and money" (Matt. 6:24b, ESV). By contrast, TV advertising teaches that happiness consists in getting the latest innovation—to an unessential product—right away.

So why do youth reared in church often leave it as soon as they can? Could it be that their hearts were molded more by the thousands of hours of such instruction from TV and other media than by the distinctly fewer hours of godly instruction from parents and pastors?

First Baptist Church

Mom and I went to the old First Baptist Church at the corner of Court and Placer Streets. Built in 1910, its shingles were weathered as dark as those of our first house on West Street. The church belonged to the mainline Northern Baptist Convention (now American Baptist Churches USA), but the pastor had been converted as an adult and preached the gospel, inviting sinners to repent and be saved.

Mom taught 6th grade girls in the Junior Department. She took me to church with her whenever the doors were open, mainly because my three older brothers would harass me if she left me home. As a result, I heard so much Sunday school teacher talk, so much Bible teaching and so many sermons that I was socialized to adults and was little influenced by my peers until I was almost out of high school.

Mom was doing her best to nurture me in the word of God and that word was affecting my behavior. Nevertheless, the conflicting heritages of my mother's Christian faith and my father's Atheism would soon collide—in me. My mother's sowing the seed of the word would bear fruit, but then the Enemy would counterattack and I would come under demonic harassment both at home and at school.

"Your adversary the devil prowls around like a roaring lion, seeking someone to devour" (1 Peter 5:8b, ESV).

4

Demonic Tactics: Harassing Thoughts

Time to Be Baptized?

When I was about 10, Mother told me that I could be baptized any time I decided I wanted to. She never pressed me to do it, but she felt that I was ready, that I "understood" the gospel. I felt no pressure about the issue, but I was a compliant child and after a while I decided that I wanted to be baptized and told the pastor. Perhaps because my mother was a Sunday school teacher, my baptism was scheduled without any counseling.

I had gone forward once at a citywide evangelistic meeting at the old Veterans Memorial Hall by the railroad tracks. There an evangelist had had people raise their hands for lots of different questions and then pressured all of us who had raised our hands to come forward. I finally went forward under the evangelist's cajoling, but I was under no conviction of sin and no one counseled me. So after praying and listening for a while to a woman calling out the name of Jesus over and over with some of the littler children, I returned to where Mom was waiting and we went home. I sensed that something was wrong with both the evangelist's pressure tactics and the lack of personal attention to many of us children who went forward. I told my mother what had happened, but I wasn't greatly troubled by it. We often had invitations at our church, but they were not high pressured and disorganized.

Mom may have made a mistake many parents make, that of thinking that their children's unforced compliance with their parents' desires by going forward at a meeting or praying a prayer means that they have been born again. Perhaps my bright child's understanding of Bible teaching misled her. Either way, I was scheduled to be baptized without having been born again. Indeed, not until I was already in the baptismal waters in our church's baptistry, did I realize two things: that the baptism was supposed to mean that I would serve Jesus for the rest of my life and that there was something in me that didn't want to do it. Faced with this conflict, I chose in my heart to serve Jesus rather than be a hypocrite because I knew that it was the right thing to do.

So no harm was done; the Spirit regenerated me, convicting me of my unwillingness to serve God. Then, by God's grace I chose to submit my life to Jesus. No one had ever explained submission to Christ as Lord to me. But from observing those with whom I have shared the gospel over the years, I have learned that even when the issue of Christ's lordship is made as clear as words can make it, sinners still often make empty professions of faith. Only the Holy Spirit can enable a sinner to truly repent by turning from self to Jesus as Lord.

Demonic Harassment: Thought Injection

After my baptism, I continued to read my Bible on my own and was happy to attend church with Mom. God had asserted his rightful place in my life. But the Scripture says, "All who desire to live godly in Christ Jesus will suffer persecution" (2 Timothy 3:12). Accordingly, some time after my baptism, out of nowhere blasphemous thoughts, including words against the Holy Ghost, came forcefully into my mind. Although such thoughts were utterly repulsive to me, I mistakenly took them to be my own and was continually stopping to ask God to forgive me. I think that my family's divided spiritual heritage left me vulnerable to this demonic mental harassment.

I mean that my father's Atheism and addiction to alcohol subjected not only him, but also his children to demonic influence. Exodus 20:5 warns parents that God visits "the iniquity of the fathers on the children to the third and the fourth generation of those who hate me" (ESV), and one of the mechanisms of this visitation may be the evil spirits that deceive and afflict God haters. I sadly conclude that as an Atheist and as one who often took God's name in vain, my father's sins affected his children through this mechanism. And, indeed, although three of us escaped it, one of my brothers suffered a lifelong addiction to alcohol.

Nevertheless, more than ever, I wanted to obey the exhortations we heard at church to witness to people about how to be saved. So despite the demonic harassment, I shared the gospel as I understood it with my friend, John. I told him that he needed to believe in Jesus so he could go to heaven when he died, and sitting on the grass in his back yard, we even prayed together. No change was apparent in John's life, but after I had prayed with him he came to realize that I was praying whenever I would stop and look at my hands while silently asking for forgiveness after a demonic blasphemy had run through my mind. Noticing my pause and concentration one day while we visited our older friend Hal, John explained to him, "He's praying." Although, mercifully, Hal made nothing of it, John's casual and unwanted exposure of my silent prayer told me that my sharing with him hadn't sensitized him to spiritual things. Apparently, nothing had come of our prayer.

At school, the hesitation my prayers for forgiveness sometimes caused in the middle of my class recitations became so apparent that my fifth grade teacher assigned me to a weekly speech therapy class where students with speech impediments practiced English pronunciation. That class included some cool sixth graders and was a rather pleasant break for me since I really had no difficulty in pronouncing words and sentences. My problem in recitation was entirely spiritual, not psychomotor.

Close is Not Enough

Although I was close to my mother, I never told her about the evil thoughts that were tormenting me. Years later she told me that she had noticed that something was wrong, but she never questioned me about it at the time, probably because of her own problems with Dad's waning devotion and growing irresponsibility in their marriage. Out of fear of going to the dentist, when younger, I had similarly concealed from her a painfully recurring toothache in a 6-year molar. As a result, I lost the tooth, which had to be pulled.

Another incident that had excited fear in me was my tonsillectomy. For some reason I was not told that I was to undergo the operation until we arrived at the doctor's office, where I was scheduled for outpatient surgery. When the anesthetic mask was put over my face I began to count as instructed, screamed for help when I smelled the ether, but then controlled myself, resumed counting and quickly lost consciousness. I still vaguely remember the ominous dream that I had while under anesthesia. That fear lingered for a while and once when I smelled something like ether under the big yellow house, I again momentarily panicked.

These fears were all part of an unhealthy pattern that isolated me from my mother when I needed her help. I don't know whether any demons gained entrance into me through these fears, but I'm convinced that the demons harassing me with evil thoughts took advantage of my fearfulness to keep me from getting Mom's help against them. Perhaps they also hindered her from asking me about my distraction.

These examples of failures of communication between my mother and me show how careful parents need to be to talk about everything with their compliant young children as well as with their not so compliant teenagers. In an individualistic culture that prizes personal independence, many children will not share their deepest anxieties even with very loving parents. But parents who not only ask questions, but who also focus full attention on their children as they answer may be rewarded with the opportunity to help their children with their troubles.

Thus, God and the devil were both hard at work in my family. Regrettably, my unbelieving father was already far gone through demonization from his drinking. By the time I was in sixth grade, the evil thoughts tormenting me had waned for no apparent reason. Perhaps my consistent response of praying for forgiveness, mistaken as it was, amounted to a resistance from which the demons eventually had to flee. But they had not given up; they merely began to exploit another, more promising area of my life. For me, the devil's work would soon begin to hinder my relationship with God, but for Dad, it would soon prove fatal.

"'The thief does not come except to steal, and to kill, and to destroy'" (John 10:10a, NKJV).

5

The Enemy Strikes

When he was around to do it, Dad was really better than Mom at comforting me when my older brothers had picked on me. He didn't try to discipline the culprits, who were beyond his control, because, I suppose, he had never taken responsibility for their discipline. But he would ask me questions about what had happened and that caused me to stop bawling so I could talk. But most of the time, he was an absent father: at work, sleeping or out drinking and gambling with his friends.

The Oldsmobile

No new cars were built for civilians during the War so a good used car was hard to get. But Dad earned good money working on Shasta Dam and happened to have enough to buy a good one when his fat friend Frank, offered to sell one to him. So in 1944, Dad paid $500 or $600 for Frank's clean, light green, 1940 Oldsmobile two-door business coupe. Dad put the car's title in Mom's name, and, of course, she wanted to learn to drive it. He let her try; but I doubt that he really wanted her to have that skill. At least, he was so impatient with her beginner's efforts at engaging the clutch of the stick shift car to start up from an uphill stop sign that she quickly got discouraged and gave up. Certainly, she was conscious of the irony of being the legal owner of a car she couldn't drive. And contemporary Feminism has, with considerable justice, made much of such oppressive ironies.

I remember Dad's going to a movie with the family at the ornate Cascade Theatre on Market Street just once. Restless, he couldn't bear to sit through the movie and left in the middle of it. I don't know what he said to Mom to excuse himself, but I felt bad when he left us. And we all knew that he just walked the block over to California Street, then lined with one bar after another for several blocks. There he could drink with his buddies at the Roosevelt Club on the corner of Placer and California Streets or play draw poker further down the street at the Old Crow Club.

The Olds was Dad's pride and joy. For him, owning and driving the Olds may have been the high point of his life. And his decline can be traced through his relationship with that car. I witnessed a wrenching episode in that decline in the early dusk of a spring evening in our big back yard. When the Olds appeared with Dad at the wheel, I was very glad to see him. But he had been drinking and as I watched he veered a little to the right and went just off the beaten track into the rain-softened earth where the weeds and spring wildflowers were beginning to grow. Instead of stopping to take measures to get traction, he kept trying to use the Oldsmobile's power to get out of the mud. The only result was that the car slipped further down the gentle slope to the right and became mired up to its hubcaps. Dad never even came in the house for dinner. He just kept racing the engine and rocking the car back and forth in the mud, converting it into a brown soup.

After dinner, to get away from the ceaseless roaring of our family car in the back yard, mother took us all downtown to a movie. As we walked up and over the Eureka Way viaduct two blocks away from home, we could still hear the whine of the engine racing its heart out under his fruitless accelerations. Next morning when Dad had sobered up, we all went out with shovels and boards and pushed the car out of the mud to dry land. We were glad when the Olds finally made it to shore (as it were), but I knew as never before how completely my dad lost his mind when drunk. Were demons working behind the wine Dad had come to depend on for solace? I have no doubt about it. Jesus said, "The thief comes only to steal and kill and destroy" (John 10:10a). In a few more years, Satan would accomplish his deadly goal in my father's life.

After the war Dad had to go farther afield to get work, and on one of these trips he rolled the Olds over. No one had seatbelts in those days, but the wreck left him and his passenger, unhurt. The Olds was still drivable, but the car's trim appearance was ruined. He never got the body work done and eventually lost the car. Near the end, Dad was reduced to driving an ancient, boxy, black Chevrolet coupe of little value and minimal performance, a car in which he could take no pride.

Family Problems and Progress—But No Breakthrough

Another incident from this period illustrates how demonically driven Dad was when drunk. I had forgotten it, perhaps repressing the memory, until my mother reminded me of it in 1998, shortly before her death, One evening when Mom, my brother Earl, Jr., and I were still seated at the dinner table, Dad came in flushed red with drink and, as he passed by, slapped Earl, Jr. I didn't even see the slap; what I do remember is the two locked together in a wrestlers' embrace on the floor.

Then, Mother commanded her son, "Let him go."

Earl, Jr., replied, "I can't; he'll hurt me."

Mother, having seized the heavy iron poker from the nearby wood stove said with determination, "He won't hurt you!" Apparently, both combatants took her threat seriously and they separated without further violence. When Dad later would threaten violence against her boys, I'm sure Mom recalled this incident.

Despite my father's descent into habitual drunkenness and gambling, Mom and Dad did manage to put together $450 to buy a small, brush-covered lot just west of the undeveloped landing approach zone north of Benton Field, a light aircraft strip on the west side of town.

The plan was for Dad and my two older brothers still living at home to dismantle the big, old-fashioned house we were renting and salvage the lumber to build a smaller house on the new site. For its lumber, then, Mom bought the old house for $500 on time payments from the Baptist church we attended. The church had bought the property where we lived on Eureka Way for their new building and, well before we moved out, was already grading the two large lots with a bulldozer and scraper.

We lived in the house my dad and brothers were dismantling until half of the new house under construction was roofed and enclosed. Fortunately, the weather was clear that fall, and my dad and brothers worked hard and fast to move the walls and lumber from the old house and rebuild them into the new. I saw little of the work because I was in school during the day and delivered newspapers afternoons. When we moved into the new house in November 1949, I had to climb a ladder to sleep in the attic because of the limited floor space ready for occupancy. I thought it was nice and cozy up there. What an adventure! Never mind that the toilet was still an outdoor privy and that we cooked on a small woodstove in half a house. It was a house of our own!

But work on the new house did nothing to moderate Dad's drinking and gambling long term. Mom and Dad were thoroughly estranged, and he was desperate enough to actually attend church once. For some reason, I wasn't there, but mother told me that the sermon dealt with sin so convincingly that, driving home after church in the old black Chevy, Dad had asked her how the preacher knew about him. Mom had to explain that the preacher didn't know anything about him personally. Nevertheless, he didn't respond to the gospel. Sadly, although the shoe fit, he refused to wear it.

Finally, Dad's threats of violence against us, her boys, drove Mom to file for divorce. She later told me that he had lost heart years before when he had realized that his lack of a high school diploma prevented him from having any chance at a supervisory position for which his knowledge and experience in the coal mines qualified him.

By His Own Hand

In the middle of the sermon in our church on the last Sunday in December 1950, Mr. Simons, the head deacon, came to the pew near the front where Mom and I were sitting. He summoned her to the foyer, leaving me there alone. A little later, he returned with a note he took up to the pastor, who paused in mid-sermon to read it. He then announced: "Our hearts are joined in sorrow with our sister, Vera Haddon, whose husband, Earl, died last night by his own hand." Later in the sermon, the pastor made the point that my father had sat in the church under his preaching of the gospel and had rejected it. And although I was shocked and numbed by the sudden, public announcement of my father's death, I was also pained by this further public revelation.

After the service, someone told me that I was to meet my mother in the tiny church office down the narrow hall between the baptistry and the bathrooms. When I entered, Mom gently asked, "Did you hear about Daddy?" When I told her of the announcement, she was not pleased, but she went on to confide in me that she had already done her grieving over Daddy when she saw that she had lost him to his drinking. I think she wanted me to understand why she wasn't crying; but then I wasn't crying either because there was relief as well as grief, even in my initial response. My father had never directly mistreated me, but in that last year, he had made Mom and me very fearful because of his violent outbursts when drunk. We were easily startled, jumpy, from the continuing fear that he might harm us. I regretted his sad end, but I knew that his tenacious unbelief in God was the root of his self-destruction.

Perhaps my dad decided to kill himself instead of carrying out his threats against the family. As a miner and driller, he knew well how to use electric blasting caps to detonate dynamite. So on that last Saturday night of 1950, he put a blasting cap into his ear and connected it to a battery. Thus, he used the skill of his drillers' trade to end his life without a disfiguring external wound.

So Dad left my mother with a 12-year-old son to raise and a house to finish building on her hourly wage as a dishwasher at the Lorenz Hotel Coffee Shop. In addition, I received $40 a month from Dad's social security benefits. But Mom had title to the lot they had bought and the house on it, so she was able get credit for building materials from Meek's Lumber Company. My brother Leonard, a natural builder, finished most of the remaining work on the house with me as an occasional helper.

One happy irony of it all was Mom's successful mastery of driving a car. She taught herself to drive with the old black Chevy, which didn't last long, and with Leonard's green 1935 Pontiac, which he left with us when he enlisted in the Air Force in 1951. Eventually she bought a two-toned, brown and beige 1946 Chevy coupe and passed the tests for a driver's license. Later on she worked for the Record Searchlight newspaper as a motor route driver using, in turn, the '46 Chevy and three new cars, a 1957 Ford, a 1961 Chevrolet and a 1973 Dodge Dart (the best of the lot). She drove 50 to 75 miles a day in summer heat, winter rains and the rare Valley snowfall every day of the year except Christmas Day to rack up close to half a million miles on the road. Smart mama, strong mama, capable mama! I love her and I miss her.

Many years later, Mom told me that what she had feared most at the death of my father was that her sons would blame her for pushing him to suicide by having filed for divorce. But Earl, Jr., and I knew too well that Dad was deranged when drunk, which by then was much of the time.

How Demons Use Worldly Sorrow

When Dad worked night shift and slept during the day, I had noticed how he used to speak to himself in short, intense, half-suppressed outbursts while lying awake in bed. Years later I found myself doing the same thing when regrets over memories of past sins against people would strike me with great emotional intensity. Often the name of the person I had hurt would involuntarily pass my lips. Now, I realize that, in my case, these intense outbursts of "worldly sorrow" sprang from a combination of guilt and regret energized by demons, just as they had previously energized the blasphemous thoughts they had injected into my mind during demonic harassment when I was 11. These intense regrets were calculated to depress and destroy me as, I believe, similar depressive thoughts finally drove my father to suicide. In *The Revenge of Conscience*, J. Budziszewski discusses such self-destructive perversion of violated conscience; he writes that repentance before God is the cure for such souls.

Dad was 50 years old when he took his life; I was then 12. The demons that for years afflicted and then finally pushed him to self-destruction probably had a similar goal in mind for me. First they would have to separate me from the God of my mother, but more of them were now free to devote full time to this project. And they already had gained a dangerous new foothold in my life.

"'But I tell you that anyone who looks at a woman lustfully has already committed adultery with her in his heart'" (Matthew 5:28).

6

Demonic Tactics: Tempting Images

As a senior in high school, my brother Parks got into trouble over some vandalism and joined the Army Air Corps in 1947. While he was home on leave a few years later, I noticed the full-page paintings of the Vargas girls in his copies of *True: The Man's Magazine*. This was not a girlie magazine; *True* had many articles on the masculine pursuits of hunting, fishing and outdoor adventure favored by my brothers. And the Vargas girls were never nude; instead, they wore bathing suits, often one-piece, but skintight.

So it was one of the seductive images of this soft-core pornography that led me to start masturbating when I was about 12. My first experiences seemed entirely wonderful; I don't remember any negative reaction. But as soon as I learned to masturbate to ejaculation, I began to experience a spontaneous revulsion. At the same time, I began to come under conviction of sin, which I believe was entirely biblical. I was certainly lusting in my heart (Matt. 5:28) for the girls and women with whose mental images I stimulated myself while masturbating.

Masturbation and Poltergeists

In non-Christian sources on the occult, I have discovered the observation that poltergeists (noise making spirits) often accompany childhood masturbation. That claim squares with my experience; I sometimes heard a scary buzz or flutter of wings in the wall next to my bed. Because I never connected my masturbation with the noise, I told my mother about it. She suggested that perhaps it was the wasps that sometimes got into the walls of the house. Then, I accepted that idea, but now I believe that the source of the noise was demonic, a poltergeist. A spirit made the noise either to harass and frighten me or to attract my attention to the spirit itself.

Fear, a Major Symptom of Demonic Influence

Another symptom of demonic activity and influence that I experienced was fear of biblical teaching about demons. During these years, we twice had a sermon on demons, once in the morning service and once in the evening. As soon as the preacher began "Incident at Gadara," I was so smitten by fear that I began reading what was printed in the bulletin to distract myself from the to-me suddenly frightful subject of demons.

I remember that sermon better than any other from my childhood. It was built on the most extreme case of demonization in the Bible, the man in Gadara (or Gerasa) occupied by a legion of demons. The motive for the sermon was our pastor's having received harassing phone calls from a local demoniac. The point was evangelistic: only by receiving Christ as Savior could you be free from the threat of sudden, arbitrary demonization.

The message was to be commended for its faithfulness to biblical revelation in its affirmation of the reality of demons at a time when the inroads of Liberalism in theology had called the very existence of Satan into question in many seminaries and churches. But it lacked the reassuring affirmation of the believer's authority over Satan (Luke 10:18-20, Ephesians. 1:19-21, 2:6) and instruction in how to exercise that authority (Matt. 4:4-10, James 4:6-8). Hearing that sermon scared me so badly that when the topic of demons was announced for an evening service a year or so later, I requested and received permission to stay home. Consequently, I didn't receive further instruction about the demons already strongly working in my life. This may be part of the reason the Scriptures so often say, "Do not fear."

The reason I was so afraid of hearing that sermon on demons before it even got started was that they already had a grip on my emotions. When I heard that the sermon was about demons, they stimulated fear in me to distract me from the sermon and to make me want to avoid further teaching on demons. Thus, I would be sure to remain ignorant both about how to discern their working in my life and about the believer's authority over demons. So, impelled by my fear, I did exactly what the demons wanted me to do. I avoided teaching on demons like the plague. The speed and power with which the demons were able to excite my fear of them makes me believe that they had already invaded my body and were working from within. Fear of and flight from biblical teaching on demons is a good sign of demonic incursion in the fearful Christian.

In contrast, the Bible counsels us to wear the full armor of God that enables us to stand firm against the devil:

> Be strong in the Lord and in his mighty power. Put on the full armor of God so that you can take your *stand* against the devil's schemes. . . . Put on the full armor of God, so that when the day of evil comes, you may be able *to stand* your ground, and after you have done everything, *to stand. Stand* firm then..."(Ephesians. 6:10-14).

Thus, in just five verses, the apostle commands us to "put on the full armor of God" twice and to "stand" four times. Why does the apostle get so repetitious about spiritual warfare? I think that the answer to this question is implied in verses 19 and 20:

> Pray also for me, that whenever I open my mouth, words may be given me so that I will *fearlessly* make known the mystery of the gospel, for which I am an ambassador in chains. Pray that I may declare it *fearlessly*, as I should.

Once again repetition. About what? About fear! When Paul is out front in spiritual warfare proclaiming the gospel, he wants people to pray for him against fear. Paul knows from his own experience that the devil's big gun is fear and that we want to run away from whatever causes it. That is why he repeats both his prayer request against fear and his exhortations for Christians to overcome fear by standing firm.

The place to begin to take your stand, then, is by seeking out sound biblical teaching on Satan, demons and spiritual warfare, especially if you find these subjects frightening. Resist Satan's use of fear to manipulate you and keep you in ignorance. He is a defeated foe, but to see him flee you must, "Resist the devil" (James 4:7b).

Masturbation: From Foothold to Stronghold

Nevertheless, neither the fear of demons nor the demons themselves are the basic problem. The world and the flesh are the avenues to the sins that demons use to get a foothold, then a stronghold in our lives. In my case, I think that my father's Atheism and drunkenness had opened the way for demons to put harassing thoughts into my mind. But I gave them a foothold only when I began to masturbate. I believe that my habitual practice of masturbation led to entry of demons into my body.

Given my earlier failures to tell anyone about either my aching tooth or the blasphemous thoughts that had bedeviled me, it's no wonder I didn't talk about masturbation with my mother or father. And my church didn't have any channel for counseling young people about masturbation either. So it became a binding habit or stronghold I was unable to break.

The resulting sin and guilt marred my fellowship with the Lord Jesus. My inability to stop masturbating after confessing it as sin left me feeling so guilty that I usually found an excuse to avoid taking the hard little square of bread and the little glass cup of grape juice that we used to symbolize the body and blood of our Lord Jesus in monthly communion. Of course, I should have received communion after confessing my sin and accepting God's forgiveness in spite of my failures. Had I persevered in the basic means of grace of confession of sin, communion, prayer, reading the Bible and attending church; the Lord would have shown me the way of escape. But this was not to be for many years.

An Ill-delivered Rebuke Releases Rebellion

Although I hadn't been attending prayer meeting for a while, one Wednesday evening, probably during the summer before I started high school, I went with Mom to the prayer meeting. My only reason for coming was that I was convicted of my sin and wanted to seek God and overcome it. That hot summer evening the group at prayer meeting was fewer than a dozen and met in a small classroom instead of using the pews in the main hall as they usually did. After the teaching, when it was time to pray, the leader looked around at the group and told us just to pray around the circle one after another. This was unusual and unexpected; usually people just prayed spontaneously in no particular order. I was very distressed because I knew that I wasn't on praying ground. When my turn came, I didn't know what else to do so I blurted out a couple of sentences. When the leader's turn to close the prayer came, he again did something unusual. In his prayer he expressed his deep grief to God over the person who had not been in the Spirit while praying.

I took this as a rebuke aimed at me and felt, first, shame; then, anger and, finally, resentment at being rebuked while seeking God by coming to prayer meeting. I didn't say anything about it to anyone, but the next Sunday when Mom told me it was time to get up to go to church, I just said, "I'm not going." Those were the most costly words I ever uttered—and the saddest. Right there I gave up 17 years of my Christian life and caused my mother and myself untold sorrow and pain.

I was wrong, dead wrong to rebel against God and the church over a leader's failure to use the biblical method of rebuke. My commitment to follow Jesus for the rest of my life was not conditioned on having perfect leaders. Nevertheless, I would say from Scripture as well as from my sad experience that public prayer should never, ever be used as a substitute for the direct, private rebuke of Matthew 18.

Growing Demonic Influence

Masturbation, then, was the wedge that had come between my Lord and me, but my rebellion in leaving the church was the sledgehammer blow that split me off from the spiritual help I needed and subjected me to even greater demonic influence. Having isolated myself from the church at 14, I was powerless against my habit of masturbation and bereft of God's guidance in making the crucial decisions about my vocation and education. Thus, the sins of masturbation and rebellion not only paved the way for my later coming under devastating demonic occupation, but also prevented me from preparing myself for the vocation suited to my talents and gifts. Instead, for nearly 20 years, I usually masturbated one or more times a day as I pursued changing, worldly academic and career goals.

I had realized early on that my masturbation with its sin of lust came between God and me. What I didn't realize until much later was that masturbation was also subjecting me to growing demonic influence. Nevertheless, and in spite of my having cut myself off from the church, I did recognize at least one demonic attack while I was still in high school. One night I was lying in bed in my room when I began to feel so fearful of some invisible presence that I got up, went to my mother's door and told her, "I feel like demons are trying to possess me!" I don't know whether she understood me, but she just told me to go back to bed. I did and whatever was causing the fear had gone. Perhaps she had prayed for me.

By trying to overpower me, the demons nearly blew their cover. Probably counting on my habitual silence, they had gone so far beyond the previous harassment of evil thoughts and scary noises and their subtle entry under cover of my sexual sin that for once I broke my silence about personal problems and asked my Christian mother for help. Had we confronted the source of the problem, which I intuitively recognized as demonic, I might have been persuaded to return to God and the church. That may be why the demons never again risked this kind of frontal assault until much later when I had been deceived into voluntarily receiving many demons.

The demons desperately want to keep the Christian ignorant of two things: 1) The believer's authority to command their departure (Ephesians: 2:6, 1:22-23; James 4:7; Matt. 4:10) and 2) God's grace through our sharing in the death of Christ that gives us victory over the sin(s) that gave the demons their foothold (Romans 6). So the demons backed off and I still didn't realize that my sin and rebellion had given them lodging in my body.

Meanwhile, a subtler form of idolatry, Nature worship, had given demons another foothold in my life. Much nobler in appearance than the grubby sensuality of masturbation, the call of the wilderness would also lead me further away from the Creator who had made the beauty of the natural world as a reflection of his own power, majesty and beauty.

"They exchanged the truth about God for a lie and worshiped and served the creature rather than the Creator, who is blessed forever! Amen" (Romans 1:25, ESV).

7

The Call of the Wild and the Call of Romance

The Call of the Wild

In late June of 1950, the summer I was 12, my brother Leonard took me backpacking into the Swift Creek basin of the Salmon-Trinity Alps Wilderness Area about 60 miles northwest of Redding. My brother was not merely teaching me woodsmanship; he was also teaching me a code of stoic toughness under the stress of wilderness travel. Patience and endurance were the primary virtues. Whenever I asked how far we still had to go, his intentionally ungrammatical reply was, "It ain't how many miles it is; it's how many days it takes."

Our scripture was not the Bible, but Robert W. Service's *The Spell of the Yukon* with its stoic and occasionally profane verse. Citations such as his challenge: "Though bad as hell the worst is, /Can you round it off with curses?" ("Code of the Lone Trail,") were common. Complaints about conditions or food were not allowed, but any problems with our feet were given immediate attention to avoid disabling blisters. The first day we walked the 8 miles from the old trailhead at Big Springs up the long Cement Creek grade and on to Parker Creek. The route roughly paralleled Swift Creek's roaring torrent of snow melt as we passed through a mixed forest of ponderosa pine, Douglas fir and California incense cedar. We crossed countless springs and small streams with grassy borders where spotted orange tiger lilies and red and yellow California columbines bloomed and Cobra-hooded California pitcher plants trapped unsuspecting flies.

I was overwhelmed by the magnificence of the red-rock and granite peaks, by the sheer beauty of Swift Creek roaring with June's snowmelt and bordered by masses of Western azalea, by the grandeur of tall trees, unspoiled forests, long meadows and high lakes. I stood in awe of nature's beauty and power. The fish and wildlife added their living charm and challenge as we vied to see who could catch the most rainbow or brook trout. Nature would soon become my first love; and, thus, for many years the creation would supplant the Creator in my life.

My First Deer Hunt

In September 1952, shortly after the beginning of my freshman year in high school, Leonard took a leave from the Air Force for a 2-week deer hunt in the mountains of Trinity County. I joined him and missed 11 days of school on the hunt. Despite the 15 days of our hunt, we didn't kill any deer. But instead of discouraging me, the experience reinforced my attachment to the wilderness and the sports of hunting and fishing.

Alone in the Wilderness

The capstone of my youthful love affair with the wilderness was my spending most of July and August 1954, the summer between my sophomore and junior years, backpacking alone in the Salmon-Trinity Alps Wilderness Area, with my brother Earl's tacit gift of his Smith & Wesson .38 Special revolver as my only companion. Becoming accustomed to solitude at 16 years of age increased my personal independence and may have contributed to the unintended and unexpected result of my never marrying.

To gain my mother's consent for this adventure, I agreed to emerge from the wilderness area weekly to get her general delivery letter with its $10 money order at the Trinity Center Post Office. Then I would mail her a card to let her know that I had survived and use the $10 to buy grub for another week. While at the store where the post office was one week, a middle aged woman in Levis offered to pay me what she could to help move her few belongings. I flatly refused, not because I didn't like to work, but because I didn't want to take a day out from being in the wilderness. I remember with regret her plaintive appeal to me, "My pack is heavy, too." My idolatrous dedication to knowing and experiencing the wilderness had hardened me emotionally as well as physically.

Academics, Economics and My First Deer

Through high school I was under the tutelage of my oldest brother, Earl. He had been drafted into the Army early in the Korean War and returned after discharge to attend Shasta Junior College in Redding and prepare for upper division work in civil engineering at the University of California (UC), Berkeley. Fresh from the army, he imposed on me a military discipline of early rising and bed making. We also headed for the wilderness to hunt deer and ski whenever we could, but his college studies limited these activities to weekends. His aversion to civilization had been moderated by his ambition to become a professional engineer.

My brother chose my high school courses to prepare me for engineering school. The math emphasis soon paid off with a job as an engineering aid for the California Division of Highways (now CalTrans) between my junior and senior years. I would work for them for the next four summers, first in the district materials lab, and later on a survey party and on construction sites in remote areas of Northern California.

Mom always let me keep all the money I earned on my own so, after my first summer's work with CalTrans, I bought a garish, green 1946 Mercury four-door sedan for $395. First day of deer season, I drove up Red Mountain above the East Fork of the Trinity River and hiked on up into the benches where Leonard and I had hunted 3 years earlier. Hunting alone that morning with brother Earl's Model 94 Winchester lever-action .30-30 carbine, I jumped two bucks and killed one of them, my first deer. On my own, I had finally completed an important family rite of passage.

The Call of Romance

Now that I had a car of my own, I started dating in my senior year in high school. I was still very shy with girls, but having been lusting after them for so long, I was eager to get closer to one of them. I didn't expect my dates to fulfill my fantasies, but the results of my interest in real live members of the opposite sex proved much more troublesome than I expected.

Things romantic were different back in the mid-50s. The pill wasn't available. Pregnancy outside of marriage was a disgrace. Abortion was illegal. Girls were expected to guard their virginity and most of us boys, for our part, were afraid to press them too far. A few couples, to be sure, had to get married, but the sexual revolution wasn't even on our horizon. A big issue was how many dates you had to have before kissing a girl goodnight. Trying to do it on the first date might result in evasive action by the girl or even no more dates with her. In 1956 many of us boys graduated high school willy-nilly as virgins. And whatever our lascivious desires, we didn't respect the few girls known to be promiscuous.

I fell hard for the younger sister of one of my friends; she was quiet and cute and when I asked for a date I was delighted to find that she liked me. But on the way home after a second or third date, I drove through the city park where some couples went to park and she quickly scooted away from me. Because I had no intention of stopping or making any advances there, I got mad at her. Later, I tried to communicate the innocence of my intentions via third parties, but that probably did more harm than good. It didn't occur to me that since she didn't know what my intentions were, I had caused her evasive response and owed her an apology for my anger about it. We had one more date, but in my self-centeredness, I never did get it and my first girl friend was gone before we really got well acquainted. Despite my intense—but superficial—emotional involvement, I had never even kissed the girl.

Disappointment Leads to Self-Indulgence

Such disappointments in life are great opportunities for Satan because our feelings of self-pity incline us to seize the disappointment as an excuse for self-indulgence. My romantic disappointment would lead me in this direction shortly, but first, the demons assigned to me would again push me a bit too far. The morning after the breakup, I lay in bed late and masturbated. Then the thought came into my mind, "I give myself to the devil." Fear and revulsion instantly seized me and I forcefully rejected the thought. That shook me up and from time to time I wondered if I had given myself to the devil. But because of my strong, spontaneous revulsion against the idea, it didn't bother me as much as it might have. What I still didn't realize was that my sexual sin had opened me up to growing demonic influence.

A few months after the breakup with my first girlfriend and with graduation approaching, I accepted an invitation to join with three of my friends to drink a couple of fifths of vodka on the weekend. I had never drunk anything before, but, sure enough, I rationalized it on the basis of my romantic disappointment. On the appointed Saturday night, the four of us all got drunk at once as we finished off the vodka we had been drinking all evening. As leading scholars at Shasta High, we thought that the brush-covered Block S Hill, which bore a large S formed of whitewashed rocks representing our school, appropriate for our antics. The experience was pleasant, and I became an occasional drinker. But it would be years before I was drunk again, and I have been drunk only about three times in my life. Because of my migraine syndrome, I sometimes got a bad hangover without even drinking very much; this may have limited my indulgence more than any concern about my father's fate. Booze would not be my undoing; sex and rock and roll music, which had just gained national prominence, were more likely avenues to self-destruction for me.

"You Ain't Nothin' but a Hound Dog"

The hip swinging Elvis Presley had just gyrated onto the American scene in 1956. His soulful rendition of "Heartbreak Hotel" and his sensual rendition of "You Ain't Nothin' But a Hound Dog" expressed my teenage sexual frustrations. The breakup of my romance had been my excuse for joining my friends in getting drunk. Rock music was another outlet.

Allan Bloom wrote in *Closing of the American Mind*:

> Rock music has one appeal only, a barbaric appeal, to sexual desire—not love, not *eros*, but sexual desire undeveloped and untutored. It acknowledges the first emanations of children's emerging sensuality and addresses them seriously, eliciting them and legitimating them, not as little sprouts that must be carefully tended in order to grow into gorgeous flowers, but as the real thing. Rock gives children . . . with all the public authority of the entertainment industry, everything their parents always

used to tell them they had to wait for until they grew up and would understand later (Simon and Schuster, Touchstone 1988, p. 73).

Bloom's description of rock as an exaltation of immature sexual impulses rings true to my experience, but he completely misses the spiritual dimensions of rock.

A Grateful Dead concert, for example, was a kind of ersatz worship experience as well as a spur to the dope use usual at their concerts and to fornication afterwards. Given the drugs and sex, demonic influence was inevitable whether or not participants consciously sought spiritual experience. Fans and foes of rock music alike recognized its intimate relation with sex and drugs

But sex, drugs and sensuous music have always been a part of Pagan religious experience. So while fans may deny it and foes like Bloom may not recognize it, the ultimate dynamic of rock is spiritual, demonic.

Christian artists have managed to tame the rock music form enough to produce many songs that I believe do honor God and through which I can joyfully worship him. This does not change the reality that the form itself, with its heavily accented back beat, evokes an anti-Christian sensuality and restlessness. Moreover, its characteristic loudness suppresses the sense of community fostered by being able to hear the voices of those singing around you. My expectation is that Christian artists will someday be inspired to discover new or recover old forms that are better suited than rock to expressing the Christian message of the kingdom of God as "righteousness, peace and joy in the Holy Spirit" (Romans 14:17, ESV).

Although rock music was a powerful engine propelling the sexual revolution and political protest, I escaped its grasp after I left Redding for UC Berkeley where cool jazz, folk and classical music were then more in fashion.

I still realized that God had a call on my life, but. "Later!" I thought. So the question was, would I somehow find Wisdom at California's great public University?

"For since, in the wisdom of God, the world did not know God through wisdom, it pleased God through the folly of what we preach to save those who believe" (1 Corinthians 1:21, ESV).

8

UC Berkeley: College of Engineering

While most of my friends with good grades were heading off to UC Berkeley, I began my studies at the local community college, now Shasta College, in the fall of 1956. I saved money and lost nothing academically by spending my freshman year at home in Redding. I socialized little and spent the nights studying hard while listening to KOBY, San Francisco, a rock music station.

Contrary to normal rules, I transferred to UC Berkeley's College of Engineering as a sophomore the next year and maintained a B+ average that year. I found the hard science and engineering theory courses of lower division engineering easy enough, but upper division courses that required getting the correct numerical answers to long computations were frustrating. I gradually realized that I had chosen the wrong academic field.

That was why I took a 6-month work-study position with San Francisco's Bureau of Engineering after the first semester of my junior year. This break in school opened the door in August 1959 for another wilderness adventure, this time in the high Sierra Nevada. In 34 days, I first walked 50 miles into the heartland of the Southern Sierras and then 230 miles north on the Muir Trail along the Sierra crest to Yosemite.

During another discouraging semester in engineering that fall, in desperation I got a recording to induce self-hypnosis to help me concentrate on my studies. Once, I almost made it into the hypnotic state, but a sudden surge of fear of demons stopped me cold. Realizing that it was my Christian upbringing that blocked my path to self-help through self-hypnosis, I resented it at the time. But now I consider that fear to have been a warning of a real danger. Indeed, to avoid demonic incursion, one should avoid passive states of consciousness—whether from hypnosis, drugs or meditative practices—because the passive mental state opens body and soul to demons.

I spent the next year working construction but finally decided to finish up in engineering to get it over with. I had dated a coed named Carla on and off from my first year at UC, but I never fell in love with her. I think that she loved me and wanted to get married, but only in my last year at UC did I realize I would regret it if I lost her. While on a winter ski tour in the Trinity Alps with my brother Leonard in December 1961, I decided at last that I would ask her to marry me. When I got back to Berkeley, however, Carla told me that she was now interested in other candidates. I was not heartbroken, but when she wrote me a nice farewell letter, I replied with a hateful letter taking my frustrations out on her. Later, when I saw and regretted my cruelty to her, the demonically energized memory of this sin against her would cause her name to cross my lips involuntarily, just as I had heard my father speak unintelligible words of distress when lying awake in bed. Thus, for years, Satan energized my regret for my sins against me. Paul tells us that such worldly sorrow brings death (2 Cor. 7:10).

My last semester in engineering was excruciating. Evenings during that spring of 1962, I would work on engineering problem sets as long as I could stand it. Then, to anesthetize the pain, I walked a few blocks down Euclid Avenue to La Val's basement beer garden for beer before bed. As I left La Val's one spring night near the end of the term, I looked up at the dark night sky and told God: "If you're there I would like to know it." Realizing that my heart had become hardened to God, I added, "But you'll have to grind me to powder." How would God respond to my request? to my challenge?

"In the middle of the journey of our life, I found myself in a dark forest, the right way was lost."—Dante.

9

Army Special Forces Volunteer

At the first big fork in the road, that of choosing my professional education, I had missed the right path and lost my way in the dark forest of life. I now realized that much, but, unlike Dante, I hadn't yet attained to midlife and was far from ready to turn around and seek the right way. I spent the summer after I finished at UC Berkeley not knowing or caring whether I had passed the courses needed to graduate. But I enjoyed working as gradechecker as I had whenever not in school since 1960.

Facing the possibility of being drafted at the age of 24, in January 1963 I joined the Army for 3 years and volunteered for Special Forces. I expected to be trained in outdoor survival. That never happened, but I did learn how to parachute out of airplanes and how to speak Spanish.

To make the risks of Special Forces duty clear, we had to sign a form agreeing that if war broke out, we would be infiltrated behind enemy lines to train and assist pro-American guerrilla forces. "Signing your life away," we called it. Unhappy about my mistake of training for the wrong profession, I was ready to throw my life away—but only in defense of my country.

I took basic and advanced infantry training at Fort Ord near Monterrey, California. There I learned to fire the vintage WW-II weapons, as well as the new M-14, an inferior rifle, and the bipod equipped A-6 machine gun. I qualified as sharpshooter, falling short of the expert rating I desired. But I did qualify as expert on the bayonet course, daily encouraged by the drill instructor's call: "What is the spirit of the bayonet?" And our response, "To kill!"

After radio school and the field exercise, instead of receiving orders for Vietnam, then viewed as a live-fire training course that many of our instructors had successfully completed, I was assigned to 8th Special Forces Action Group at Fort Gullick, Canal Zone (Panama). This meant 3 more months at Fort Bragg for training in spoken Spanish. Given my natural talent for language, I enjoyed studying Spanish 5 and a half days a week. Indeed, I was so arrogant about it that I told a fellow student that I expected to be honor graduate, a boast I fulfilled.

From Sea to Shining Sea by Motorcycle

On graduation from the language course late in May 1964, I left Fort Bragg on my Honda 250cc Scrambler to cross the country in nine days. In the Colorado Rockies on the old Highway U. S. 40, I crossed the Continental Divide three times in two days, encountering wet snow on the third crossing at Muddy Pass in early June. Several days later I crossed the Sierra Nevada over Donner Pass and on reaching the hot Sacramento Valley at Roseville was halted by a burned out piston, the first of two pistons to blow during my 30-day leave.

After the Honda shop in Redding replaced the first blown piston, I visited my friends in Berkeley. There, I tried marijuana for the first (and last) time, avidly inhaling on the last joint that was being passed around the room with appropriate jazz on the stereo. The high point of my leave was a night ascent of the west suspension tower on the San Francisco side of the Bay Bridge with my friend Tim, whom I'd met in the Cal Hiking Club while still a student. The low points were laying my motorcycle down in eucalyptus leaves on a curve in the road in the Berkeley Hills near Tilden Park one night and later burning out the second piston on Interstate 80 near Vallejo. There I lost my traveling bag complete with my military orders to Panama and my pay records.

Still Lost in the Dark Woods

What I most regretted was the loss of the books I had bought in Berkeley and one in particular. For I had at last obtained my own personal copy of Robert W. Service's *The Spell of the Yukon*, with its gritty poems setting forth the stoic code of the North that required a man to fight on, grimly defying his inevitable defeat and death by the harsh forces of nature.

This inauspicious ending to my leave in California didn't awaken me to the reality that I was still lost in the dark woods without any idea of what spiritual forces were guiding me or of where they were bent on taking me. Geographically, I was headed for Panama, Puerto Rico and Peru; places where I would gain good fluency in Spanish and broaden my cultural horizons, putting me on the path of new academic and career ambitions.

U. S. Canal Zone, Panama, Puerto Rico, Peru

The Panama Canal Zone was OK by me, but not to some of my fellow Green Berets, who even volunteered for duty in Vietnam to cut short their 18-month tour in Panama. Others went there later and at least one of their names is on the black marble wall of the Vietnam Veterans Memorial in Washington.

I was assigned to "E" Company, the signal or communications company of 8th Special Forces Action Group at Fort Gulick in the U. S. Canal Zone. Being in the signal company meant that I would not be on a 12-man "A" team that would be trained in the jungle in guerilla and counter-guerilla tactics. I took the disappointment in stride, resigned to the army's ways and realizing that there wasn't much I could do about it.

When we arrived in the Canal Zone in June 1964, the Republic of Panama was still off limits to us because of the flag riots of the previous January that had killed 21 people. This only meant greater freedom for the troops to go to the off-limits clubs with prostitutes because the MPs were not on their usual patrols in town. I joined a friend from Fort Bragg in visiting Club Zamba where I discarded my virginity with a prostitute. Since this kind of sex didn't satisfy me, I spent a lot of off-duty time sitting in the on-limits clubs talking to the bar girls but never buying them their expensive, probably non-alcoholic drinks. Since I could speak Spanish, I could get some free conversation. I also visited prostitutes in Panama City and in another town a few times and could well have suffered some demonic transference from them, but, if so, I didn't notice it.

I used Benzedrine a couple of times; you could purchase it at any drug store in Panama. I tried it because I remembered Jack

Kerouac's glowing portrayal of using bennies while hitchhiking up the California coast highway in *The Dharma Bums*, which I had read while in Berkeley. But my experience with it was bad, especially, the time I took it to increase my alertness during a communications alert in the middle of the night. I was wide awake and wasn't too messed up to operate a radio, but I felt awful. Never again! Alcohol, whose dangerous effects I knew all too well from my father's example, would remain my occasional drug of choice. Use of drugs (biblical *pharmakeía, sorcery* [NIV]) and abuse of alcohol are frequent avenues for demonization, but I don't believe that my limited use of them opened me up to demons. They gained their stronghold in me mainly through sexual sin.

El Peru: Lima, Cuzco, Macchu Picchu

I took a 30-day leave to tour Peru and after arriving in Lima visited Cuzco and Macchu Picchu, considered by occultists to be one of the spiritual power points of the hemisphere. But I was ignorant of its spiritual reputation and just wanted to see the lost city of the Incas, with its impressive stonework. Although I made a solo walk through a little tunnel out to a point, all I got was a good look at some very steep ground plunging downward to the Urubamba River far below. The spirits purported to lurk at Macchu Picchu left no impression on me.

Where to Next?

In August 1965, President Johnson made a major speech promising further military aid to South Vietnam. We listened closely to our Commander-in Chief and, reading between the lines, I realized he was going to order a big buildup in U.S. forces there. Given the Army's large investment in my training, it only made sense for them to extend my enlistment for a year and send me to Vietnam. I had never intended to make a career of the Army, but if the President declared a National Emergency, he could certainly extend our enlistments. Frustrated by having prepared for the wrong career at the University, my response had been the *beau geste* of volunteering for hazardous military duty. It seemed that the time had come to make good on that gesture. So I took it for granted that I was headed for combat in Vietnam and began to adjust my mind to it in advance. After all, what had I been trained for over the last 3 years?

"Good and ill have not changed since yesteryear; nor are they one thing among Elves and Dwarves and another among Men. It is a man's part to discern them, as much in the Golden Wood as in his own house"—Aragorn (J. R. R. Tolkien, The Two Towers, *Ballentine, 1965, p 50).*

10

Tolkein's Trilogy Resonates with Truth

UC Santa Barbara

I was surprised that, instead of extending the enlistments of trained personnel like me, the Johnson Administration just increased the draft levies to build up the Army's ranks. This left me free to return to school on my veteran's benefits. Although in August I had not even expected to be discharged for more than a year, I was released from Fort Jackson, South Carolina, 16 days early on December 23, 1965. I hit civilian ground running, and by January 1966, I was enrolled as a Spanish major at the University of California, Santa Barbara (UCSB). My plan was not to get a second bachelor's degree in Spanish, but to round out my education in the humanities to prepare for the Foreign Service Exam and become a diplomat in the U. S. Department of State. I was still going my own way; however, military discipline had not touched the inner core of my independence from God and man.

Back to the Wilderness

That summer of 1966, I didn't get work out of the union hall until August so I worked on through December as gradechecker on a road down the Klamath River in a remote mountain area of Northwestern California near the town of Happy Camp. One weekend I went hunting alone on the mountain above Seiad, a smaller town upstream. There I killed a deer not too far from the road. Not wanting to bother to return to my pickup for my bone saw and backpack, I gutted the deer and made a kind of backpack of it by putting the forelegs through a slit in the skin covering the tendons of the hind legs. But the deer was heavier than I thought, and when I got under the weight of the carcass and began to rise, its weight crushed me back to the ground. I became irrationally angry, indeed, enraged. Great were my curses and blasphemies. I probably also put some vertebrae out of place in my neck and may have done some injury to my lower back. When I calmed down, I fetched the needed gear from the pickup, skinned the deer, sawed it in two and carried it back in my backpack in two trips. Shortly afterwards, however, I developed a severe crick in the neck and headaches that would plague me for years.

Eventually, I consulted a neurosurgeon and neurologist about the headaches. The surgeon thought I might have an aneurism (ballooning) of a blood vessel in the brain, but the neurologist who reviewed my electroencephalogram said that I was a migraine type but didn't have an aneurism. He added that he, too, had headaches and advised me not to consult any more surgeons because one might cut on me just to see if he could find out what was causing the headaches. Made sense to me, so I learned to live with the headaches until they were relieved, in part by chiropractic, in part by faith in Christ. My extreme anger and my blasphemies when crushed to the ground by the deer carcass could well have resulted in further demon incursion, but I can't say for sure.

High Culture and Low Sensuality

Before the close of the summer season, I drove up to Ashland, Oregon, on a couple of weekends for some of the plays at the Shakespearean Festival there. Drama and literature were beginning to vie with Nature as objects of my devotion.

I also had a few sexual encounters with young women in the "liberated" atmosphere of the late sixties, but my independence and arrogance kept me from developing any close relationships with them. Meanwhile, I continued my incessant habit of masturbation while avoiding pornography and sexually stimulating movies as unsatisfying.

Frodo Lives!

J. R. R. Tolkien's *The Hobbit* and *The Trilogy of the Rings* were the most positive influences I encountered at UCSB. "Frodo Lives!" posters with their strange pink and blue plants and creatures were abundant and piqued my interest. During the summer, I read the books because they were so popular with the undergraduates, much as I had read *The Stranger* as a student in Berkeley. But somehow the Christian themes of endurance, self-sacrifice and Providence pervading these books unconsciously resonated with me as Camus's Existentialism never did. Still, it was quite a while before I consciously recognized the Christian worldview of Tolkien's tale of Middle-earth. And the themes of how God uses the weak to confound the strong and even the evil to accomplish his good purposes escaped me until well after my re-conversion to Christ about 4 years later.

J. R. R. Tolkien and Providence

But then, I came to understand the overarching yet unobtrusive Power that works its inscrutable will throughout Tolkien's history of Middle-earth's Third Age. The slender evidences of the existence of this Power give hope, but never assurance of victory, to the elves, men, dwarves and hobbits who struggle against the ever growing might of the Dark Lord Sauron and his evil empire of Mordor.

This theme of Providence first appears early in *The Fellowship of the Ring* when the good wizard Gandalf describes to Frodo, the Ringbearer, the conflicting powers of good and evil at work in bringing the evil One Ring of Power to light. He goes on to tell Frodo that the good power *meant* for Frodo to receive the Ring. Later at the Council of Elrond, elven King Elrond explains to the leaders who happen to be at his palace, "'the purpose for which you are called. Called, I say, though I have not called you to me. . . . You have come . . . by chance as it may seem. Yet it is not so. Believe rather that it is so ordered that we . . . must now find counsel for the peril of the world.'"

So two of the wisest and most powerful of the leaders of the forces of good in Middle-earth insist from the beginning that they serve the purposes of a transcendent goodness. And when the quest that begins in *The Fellowship of the Ring,* continues in *The Two*

Towers and finally concludes in *The Return of the King*; Tolkien's tale has revealed a hidden Power so mighty that it assigns the physically weakest of its friends to the most difficult task, so wise that it uses its enemies as well as its friends to fulfill that quest, and so patient that its irresistible momentum in fulfilling its purposes is scarcely visible to mortals.

But that understanding was to come only later. Meanwhile, with my biweekly fix of history, rationality and literary culture from *National Review*, I clung to the hope of political salvation through Conservative politics. Perhaps some of NR's writers knew better than that and their faith, too, may have affected me. In any case, my new career ambition would soon be tested by the Foreign Service's two-step combination of stiff written and oral exams for would-be Foreign Service Officers.

"Behold, the nations are like a drop from a bucket and are accounted as the dust on the scales" (Isaiah 40:15, ESV).

11

Washington, D. C.: State Department

Foreign Service Exam

After finishing three terms at UCSB, I decided I had enough of Spanish, French, philosophy, English literature, and art and music appreciation to take on the Foreign Service Exam. So I took the written exam in San Francisco on a sunny day in early December 1967, and my score qualified me for the crucial oral exam in March. While waiting for this exam, I moved from Redding to a seedy hotel on Shattuck Avenue in downtown Berkeley. At the Roos-Atkins men's clothing store just off the UC Campus on the South Side, I paid about $100 for a brown wool suit for the big occasion.

At my oral exam, I was seated at the foot of a long table with three examiners way down at the other end at a shorter table that formed the top of a "T." Again, the exam results were favorable, as I learned in the State Department's letter to me of March 22. I was pleased because many students across the country spend their academic careers preparing for the exam in prestigious universities with a reputation for preparing successful candidates, but only a small percentage of those taking the exams are successful.

The assassination of Martin Luther King, Jr., in April of 1968 found me still in Berkeley where I cautiously avoided the rioting that broke out in the wake of King's death. I think that I returned to Redding later that month for the start of the construction season.

I again lived in Ashland, Oregon, and worked on interstate highway construction in Northern California. An FBI investigator interviewed me in my Siskiyou Boulevard apartment in Ashland for my security clearance. As I had expected, his investigation turned up nothing damaging so I received a letter from the Department of State, dated July 3, 1968, telling me I was eligible for appointment as Foreign Service Officer. The bad news was that the Department's budget would not permit appointment before the summer of 1969 (fiscal 1970) and there was no guarantee even then. They did suggest that I apply for the federal Management Intern Program for which my status on the Foreign Service list fully qualified me. But I had no interest in being a federal bureaucrat unless it was with the State Department.

A Review for *National Review*

That same 4th of July weekend of 1968, I spent writing a book review of Jean-Jacques Servan-Schreiber's *The American Challenge* for *National Review*. The long weekend had given me just enough time to compose and type up the review on my Smith-Corona manual typewriter before I had to get back to work as a gradechecker on Interstate 5, Monday morning. This was the first article I had ever submitted for publication and I mailed it in without even making a copy of the manuscript. To my delight, my review appeared in *National Review* two months later on September 10.

When construction shut down that winter, I returned to my mother's place in Redding. Directionless as I was, I happened to read in my *National Review* an advertisement for a scholarship in an interdisciplinary graduate program in Politics and Literature at a small, private university in Texas. The program blurb suggested the possibility of knowledge of moral absolutes. I was intrigued and sent for an application.

Mexico by Plane, Bus, Train

Having saved money as I usually did while working, I set aside $600 or so for a trip to Mexico. My plan was to return to the States by way of Texas to visit the University there for a scholarship interview. So in January 1969, I took a 3-week vacation trip through Mexico. Returning from Mexico City I went north to Guanajuato, then to San Miguel de Allende and finally, by overnight train through the desert, to Nuevo Laredo across the border from Laredo, Texas.

From there I traveled to the University of Dallas in Irving, Texas, for my scholarship interview. I learned that the philosophies of the faculty ranged from the Aristotelianism of the followers of Leo Strauss through Southern traditionalism to ultraconservative Catholicism. Unfamiliar as I was with the details of some of their philosophies then, I thought that compared to the barbarianism of the New Left and the Marxism of the Old Left, they were on the side of the angels. But the interview did not prepare me for the sudden appearance 3 years later of Dr. Eric Voegelin as a visiting professor teaching Greek political thought. By then, Voegelin's skepticism about the bodily resurrection of Jesus Christ would be for me unacceptable.

Washington, D. C.: India Desk

Late that January the State Department was finally able to offer me an appointment as a Summer Intern. So early in June 1969, I left Redding by car for Washington, DC, for my stint as an intern on the India Desk. Before leaving California, I took a short backpacking trip up the Merced River. It was the first time I had been in Yosemite since my trek up the John Muir Trail from Mineral King a decade earlier in September 1959. Then I came down by a Merced River that was a gentle stream; now in June I climbed up by a raging torrent hurtling down its granite bed and flooding the trail where the river spread out along flatter reaches. Only last summer, three hikers fell into those waters and were swept over the falls to their deaths. In this world, both spiritual and physical realities have their deadly hazards, but the spiritual hazards are usually well concealed.

I arrived in Washington to go on the federal payroll on June 16, 1969, not long before America's first moon landing. I found an apartment in Arlington, Virginia. Traffic on the beltway and in Arlington was heavy, but the traffic circles in DC itself were the worst for the uninitiated. These are made necessary by the diagonal streets that intersect the square grid of the rest of the streets. The diagonals and squares of a plan view of the city, however, together make a pattern of a compass and square (the symbols of Masonry) encompassing the major government buildings. This reflects the occult Masonic philosophy of the French architect of this planned city. I learned of this occult influence in our nation's capital only many years later while on a mission in La Plata, Argentina. This town was founded by a Mason and had the same evil symbolism worked into the architecture of its plan.

At the State Department, I was assigned to the India desk in Washington and for some reason did a background study on Sikkim, then a small buffer state on India's northern border south of Tibet and between Nepal and Bhutan. Sikkim was known to most Americans if at all only because American heiress Hope Cooke had married Sikkim's prince and was queen of the land for a while. Later I read in *National Geographic Magazine* of how one of Sikkim's rulers in his old age stopped his friendly intercourse with the spirits of the religion of his Lepcha people because the spirits were too demanding. In my own experience, I would find dismissing the spirits I had intercourse with much more difficult. The spirits are, indeed, demanding, but they want to consume their enemies—Christians—completely.

By the late 60s, it seemed obvious to those with a Conservative perspective that American popular and political culture were off track. The University of Dallas's Willmoore Kendall Program in Politics and Literature offered me the opportunity to seek in political philosophy and literature an answer to the question of where the American experiment had gone wrong. Knowing the answer to that question seemed to me to be far more important than having a prestigious career in the Foreign Service promoting the policies of a nation of increasingly uncertain character. So by the time the State Department finally offered me the appointment as Foreign Service Officer in July 1969, I had already received my scholarship and decided to begin my graduate study in the interdisciplinary program in political philosophy and literature in Texas. While there, I would encounter even more than I had expected of both good and evil.

"For thus says the Lord God, 'Behold, I, I myself will search for my sheep and will seek them out'" (Ezekiel 34:11, ESV).

12

Politics, Literature and God

I left Washington for Texas to begin school in mid-August, but I was halted before I even got out of Virginia when a bearing on a rear axel of my '56 Chevy went out. Then a young man who said he could get me a used axel came by the gas station where I was stranded. I paid him 10 bucks for it, installed it and was back on the road before dark. This Providence then went unappreciated but was very helpful since my salary as an intern had been much less than my usual wage as a union grade-checker.

Once in Texas, I found an apartment several miles from the University of Dallas. Among both faculty and students, Conservative Christian and Classical perspectives predominated in this doctoral program in political philosophy and literature, but a few of the students were quite skeptical. During the first semester, in Politics we had Modern Political Theory (Machiavelli) and Ancient Political Theory (from Cicero to Augustine). In Literature we had The Epic and The Novel to 1900.

Despite my success in writing for *National Review* the previous year, I had to refine my research skills. In our courses, we read many of the classic works of Western literature and a smaller number of the basic works of political philosophy. In addition, we usually wrote a major paper for each of the four courses. Cooking for myself and not getting any exercise, I lost about 6 pounds that semester. To save time, I moved into the undergraduate dormitory on campus, giving me more time to study and to talk with people.

The University was Roman Catholic and many students took their faith seriously. Among these in my graduate program were Carl, who became my friend and confidant, and Jon, an earnest second-year student. In self-defense, I rightly called myself a backslidden Baptist rather than the NP (No Preference) that had been recorded at my request on my military dog tags. Accordingly, that Easter I went to a Southern Baptist Church in town. I appreciated their enthusiasm and confident affirmation of faith, but my heart was unmoved by the service.

In the college library, however, I found a passage in an obscure book in which the author, an elderly priest, had the audacity to affirm that God's creation of Adam and Eve as the original pair of human beings was quite reasonable. I didn't read the rest of the book, but this affirmation encouraged me to be more open to faith because I realized that a faith divorced from the biblical account of creation would be unreasonable. Now I see that I was looking for a knowledgeable and educated writer who would affirm the reasonableness of the biblical account from Creation to the Second Coming. Although I had attended a Baptist church into my teens, I hadn't the faintest idea of where to look for such a reasoned apologetic. Today, Christian apologists and Bible teachers such as Lee Stroebel, Ravi Zacharias, William Lane Craig, Erwin Lutzer and R. C. Sproul fulfill this need with intellectual excellence and cultural awareness.

In a spring semester course, The American Novel, we read a lot of William Faulkner's novels and one by Robert Penn Warren, *All the King's Men*. The narrator, Jack Burden, is a history student turned journalist who becomes a political aid to a populist southern governor modeled on Louisiana's Huey Long. Fleeing his disillusion with politics, Burden drives west from Louisiana to California, a pilgrimage from which he returns to finally come to terms with his family history, including his father's suicide. I don't remember whether I noticed the parallel with my own father's suicide, but as I set out from Texas after a successful academic year, I had a premonition that my similar journey westward across the desert to California was freighted with some great significance. I still had no idea what that meaning or purpose might be, but I would find out when I reached my journey's western end in Santa Barbara, California.

"Then Jacob asked him, 'Please tell me your name'"
(Genesis 32:29a, ESV).

13

Back to the Faith, May 1970

Tears form in my eyes and quickly dry on my face in the warm desert air. I am driving my two-toned blue, 1956 Chevrolet hardtop west across the New Mexico desert towards California one Sunday late in May. On the radio, a preacher is talking about Jacob's insistence on knowing the name of the Angel of the LORD with whom he was wrestling. Since the Angel really was God, the message is that we, like Jacob, need to know God's name, to know who he is and to have a relationship with him. That sermon pierces my heart, because I know it is true. Nevertheless, I don't call on God there alone in the desert.

Instead, when I get to Santa Barbara, I call up Laura, a young woman I had met at UCSB while studying Spanish and had taken out to dinner while passing through on my way to Texas the previous December. She is really hurting because she has recently broken off with a serious boyfriend. I realize that her guilt is more than a bad feeling and needs real forgiveness, but I also know that I am too far from God to help her find him.

So after we hang up, I finally do what I have to do. Alone in my Motel 6 room, I kneel there beside my bed. I haven't prayed much for a long time, but I remember that you approach God through his Son, Jesus. I ask the Father to forgive me for failing to keep my childhood commitment to follow Jesus, and when I stand up, I know that I have been forgiven. Life will never be the same again.

The Holy Spirit Moves Across the Land

Focused on my graduate studies at a private university, I had heard nothing of the Jesus Movement among the hippies on both Coasts nor of the revivals that had broken out at Christian colleges such as Asbury in Kentucky and Azusa in California. Nor had anyone personally confronted me with God's word. Nevertheless, I had been picked up by the same move of the Holy Spirit that was sweeping across the country, touching college students and hippies alike.

When I got home to Redding, I didn't tell my mother what had happened; I wanted to surprise her. So the next Sunday, I showed up for morning services at her church and found her in the lobby. She seemed to take my arrival in stride, whether as an expected answer to prayer or out of a diffidence born of long endurance of disappointment at my past failures to honor her and her faith, I don't know.

My concern for Laura's salvation was integral to my re-conversion to the faith and this concern carried over to others, beginning with my own family. After waiting a while to make sure I was stable in my faith, I wrote to each of my three older brothers telling them of my return to faith in Christ and recommending him to them, too.

Back to the Bible

·I bought a copy of the New English Bible (NEB) and knew from the years I had attended church that I should begin by reading the foundational books of Genesis and Romans. And I recognized the Modernism of the NEB's "Once upon a time" introduction to Genesis 11, because the pastor of my childhood church had often told us how he had bucked the unbelieving, Modernist or Liberal professors at his seminary. He had been a stockbroker before his conversion and only then went to seminary. As a man of the world soundly converted, he was unimpressed by the skepticism of theologians who didn't believe in the God of the Bible. So in spite of my having abandoned the church he pastored, his teaching benefited me when I finally returned to the faith.

That summer was idyllic. I joined my mother's independent Baptist church and soaked up the Bible teaching. I still remember the moment when, standing in my mother's backyard looking through the blue oaks at the red sun setting in the west, I sensed that my relationship with the Creator put me into a new harmony with his creation. I no longer worshiped it as I had when fleeing from God, but I had at last found my rightful place within it. As a servant of the Creator, I could enjoy it in submission to its moral and physical order revealed by both Scripture and the creation itself. I was much less aware that the kingdom of God had not yet come in its fullness, that the cosmic war between God and Satan was still raging

How Do You Resist the Devil?

But at the Christian bookstore in town, I found a booklet with these words written in white across the black cover: "Do You Know How to Resist Satan?" The author, G. W. Excel, told how to follow the example of Christ in his Temptation (Matt. 4:1-11) by recognizing satanic thoughts when they abruptly popped into one's mind, by then rebuking Satan in the name of Jesus, and finally by responding as Jesus did with Scripture. It made sense to me, perhaps because I recalled my childhood experience of harassment by demons who had injected their evil thoughts into my mind. So I memorized Matthew 4:10: "Get thee hence Satan, for it is written, 'Thou shalt worship the Lord thy God, and him only shalt thou serve'" (KJV); and I began to use it. This practice would prove to be more important to me than I could imagine.

Beyond Screwtape

Most readers of C. S. Lewis are aware from his portrayal of the demonic correspondence of Wormwood and his "uncle" Screwtape in *The Screwtape Letters* that Lewis took the efforts of demons to mislead Christians quite seriously. Moreover, in the second volume of Lewis's space trilogy, *Perelandra*, a couple of incidents illustrate his recognition that demons have the ability to inject thoughts into our minds. In the first chapter, a Christian friend of the novel's hero, Ransom, sets out to aid him in his mission to save the planet Venus (Perelandra) from diabolical machinations. But Ransom's friend encounters a demonic mental "barrage" that nearly diverts him from his rendezvous with Ransom at his country cottage (pp. 11-20).

I would comment that a confident verbal rebuke of Satan in the name of Jesus will usually cut such mind battles short. And, indeed, near the end of the book, Ransom himself, in response to the intellectual doubts "poured into his own mind by the enemy's will," finally recognizes their source and rebukes the devil by yelling, "Get out of my brain. . . ." (Ch. 14, p. 181). This clearly shows Lewis's grasp of the spiritual battle that rages for the control of our minds.

Hear What the Holy Spirit Says

At the time, things were looking great to me both spiritually and academically. My first year's achievement in my graduate program suggested that I had finally found my vocation as a college teacher. But Satan was not about to let me go that easily, and God would permit him to test me. I didn't realize how vulnerable to demonic deception my mixed spiritual heritage and history of sexual sin had left me. I was just becoming aware of the spiritual warfare long raging around me and was still dangerously ignorant about it. I needed to listen most attentively to the voice of the Holy Spirit to avoid becoming a battle casualty—which is exactly what happened when I disregarded the warning voice of the Spirit and received another "Jesus" as told in the next chapter.

Part 2: Open Warfare

"But the Spirit saith expressly, that in later times some shall fall away from the faith, giving heed to seducing spirits and doctrines of demons" (1 Timothy 4:1, RV, 1901).

14

Spiritual Seduction
Receiving Another "Jesus"

"It's Jesus," is the thought that hits me almost immediately after I go to bed one night early in June not long after arriving back home in Redding. Simultaneously with the thought, I feel a powerful sensation of love. At once I realize two things: that a spiritual presence has approached me and that it may not be of God.

As a child I had heard in church that you could test the spirits by their response to a verbal formula about the blood of Jesus. So I ask, "Do you come in the blood of Jesus?" I sense no reply and eventually go on to sleep. But for a few nights the spirit persists with the same tactic. Finally, when I again ask the spirit whether it comes in the blood of Jesus, I feel a deeper intensity of the sensation of love. I take this as my answer: the combination of love and Jesus seems too sweet to reject and I accept the spirit as "Jesus."

I am completely deceived by the enemy's two-pronged attack on my mind and my senses. The thought that the spirit is "Jesus" is a demonic lie injected into my mind. And the sensation of love is a sensual, physiological response stimulated, I believe, by a spirit already lodged in my body as a result of my habitual masturbation. But the sexual basis of this sensation is veiled, especially at first.

Masturbation's Demonic Stronghold

But how could an evil spirit gain the right to use my body against me in this way? The answer is that although I had been delivered from masturbation and had not sinned sexually during the short time I had been back in fellowship with the Lord, I had masturbated continually during the previous 20 years. Secular psychologists and even many Christian counselors consider this normal and harmless, but my experience of masturbation was sinful if gauged by Jesus' words, "Anyone who looks at a woman lustfully has already committed adultery with her in his heart" (Matthew 5:28). And certainly, I was lusting for the women whose images I fantasized during masturbation. My conviction that my masturbation was sinful was so strong that I felt myself unfit for communion and this despite my not having received any teaching about masturbation in church.

Indeed, masturbation had been crucial in breaking my fellowship with the Lord as a teenager. Moreover, although I didn't realize it, this sin had given evil spirits access to my body. Thus, I had already received a demon or demons of lust into my body without realizing it. At the opportune time, from this beachhead they were able to launch a new tactic of deception by which they gained my unwitting cooperation in expanding their occupation to all parts of my body, including, finally, even my brain.

I don't know just when demons first took up residence in my body, but I believe it was in my youth after I began to masturbate. Later, during my years of backsliding, I became conscious of what I now believe were demonic experiences after masturbation. Sometimes I had a somewhat disturbing, but perversely pleasant sense of chaos; other times I felt enveloped with a pleasant sensation of oneness with myself in the darkness. Passivity to the point of not moving my body at all was essential to maintaining the pleasant sensation, and I realized that something different was happening to me. But I imagined that these were merely occasional physiological side effects of masturbation. Only after my consciously spiritual experiences of the demonic—both the titillating and the terrifying—did I discern that these previous experiences, too, had been demonic. Thus, my vulnerability to further occupation by consciously receiving deceiving spirits grew out of my previous unconscious reception of demons through my sin of lust committed in masturbation.

As my new spiritual experience progressed, I sensed a spiritual presence about me even during the day. While driving my car I felt pleasant, tingling sensations in my skin at different places on my chest and a trembling in the flesh about my waist. But the sensuous stimulation I received in bed at night became so irresistible that at least once I went to bed in the middle of the day to enjoy it. Of course, it came to my mind as the Lord's wanting me to be there for him to show me his love. Obviously, I was a particular favorite of the Lord Jesus!

By the time I left Redding for Texas in late August, I was experiencing a sense of elation at times during the day. I attributed this to the Spirit of God rather than to the flesh and the devil and took it to be the result of my return to faith in Christ. Back at school in Texas, my shirts began to cling to the skin of my chest and torso at certain points with a mild burning sensation that continued for most of the day. At night, the spirits took on the role of the "Bridegroom" in earnest, and I that of the "Bride" of Christ: they moved my body in an imitation of sexual intercourse, still without orgasm.

I don't believe that the spirits take any pleasure in sex; for them it was just a means to gain entrance to my body. Thus, not just one, but many different spirits gained my consent and cooperation in taking up residence in my body. Although the spirits stimulated me to erection, their stimulation never led to ejaculation, which might have blown their cover.

Medieval demonologies call such "sexual" spirits incubi (male) and succubi (female) according to their sexual role. I can't vouch for the details of the ancient accounts, but I can testify that incubi are not merely a medieval superstition. They are a real and present spiritual danger, especially to spiritual Christians who are seeking deep spiritual experiences of God through mysticism, especially, bridal mysticism. The obvious perversity of bridal mysticism for me as a heterosexual male only illustrates the overriding power of spiritual deception.

Goal of the Occupiers: The Brain

I didn't realize that my body was being occupied by evil spirits, but they were pressing into it either directly or through an orifice, such as the nasal passage, which was their major focus. And despite my total cooperation and passivity before their onslaught, entry was not as easy for the spirits as might be expected from some presuppositions about matter and spirit. There seems to be a spirit-body barrier—at least with a Christian—that can be breeched only gradually or with some difficulty. They had to press hard to enter the brain in particular. My calendar for October 31, 1970, for example, has this note: "Nasal pressure so intense I reject the experience. . . ." For the spirits, the nasal passage was important, I believe, as a direct avenue to the brain through which they could suppress the mind and control the body. Unfortunately, I didn't keep up my rejection of the spirits and returned to surrendering myself to them. When in November or early December, they finally managed to breech the barrier to the brain, I felt a stinging sensation inside my skull and thought, "If this isn't the Holy Spirit, I'm in real trouble."

Well, it wasn't and I was. The sudden onset of overwhelming fear on that fateful December night in the dorm recounted in Chapter 1 followed closely on this stinging demonic entrance into my brain. I was so utterly deceived that I had thought I was walking in faith and obedience. But I was beginning to realize that I had somehow blown it when that kindly Hungarian gentleman shared 1 Peter 4:12-13 with me. Although I couldn't apply this Scripture because it was my sin that led to my suffering, I finally had to do just as Peter counseled in 1 Peter 4:19: "Let those who suffer according to God's will entrust their souls to a faithful Creator while doing good" (ESV).

Somehow I made it through my final exams and caught a flight from Love Airport in Dallas to San Francisco and from there on home to Redding for Christmas vacation. As a former airborne troop, I had little fear of flying, but that flight was a fearful one because of the spiritual battle raging within me.

Satan Unmasked: From Uncertainty to Total Resistance

Back at home in Redding, I found the spiritual presences again friendly, and in my confusion I accepted them at least once more.

But 2 days before Christmas, I began resistance to them again, still uncertain about what was going on. Then, according to a note on my calendar for Monday, December 28, I awoke that morning "deranged, loins [thighs] trembling."

My mother wisely arranged for me to see an older Baptist pastor later that day, and I told him my story. Pastor Smith gently replied that my leading symptom of fear was itself diagnostic of Satan's work, "Satan's calling card," he called it. And he gave me a copy of the third volume of Watchman Nee's *The Spiritual Man* for guidance on how to recover. In addition, he warned me that the kind of false spiritual experience Nee describes takes time and effort to overcome. Finally, he prayed for me. Some days later he took me with him to a meeting of the pastors of his denomination in the area, not for group ministry, but just to give me some support. Thus, this wise old pastor set me straight on the source of my experiences, gave me hope, warned that my recovery might be arduous and long, prayed for me and extended unusual fellowship to me. Of all the pastors from whom I sought counsel, he was the wisest and the most helpful, a model to be emulated.

After that meeting, I marked my calendar with a capital "R" for "Resistance" Day because from that day on I began to consistently reject and resist the evil spirits without and within. Now at least, I had clear direction. It still seemed incredible to me that a Christian could fall under such demonic influence while doing so many things right. But once I recognized the basic deception, everything began to fall into place. I realized that the Holy Spirit had tried to warn me when I first encountered the, counterfeit spirit of Jesus, 6 months earlier. Then, I had wondered whether or not this presence might be demonic. That question in my mind certainly had come from the Holy Spirit, but, unfortunately, I disregarded his gentle voice.

Although I now opposed them, the spirits inside me considered themselves right at home and even those outside didn't retreat at once. Indeed, things got much worse. I never did see the spirits, but in the darkness one night soon after I began to resist them, I sensed a large, winged presence with claws pressing into me. Terrified, I fled my bedroom and tried to sleep on the couch in the living room with the lights on. This was better, but although I was exhausted, the spirits within kept me awake by jerking the muscles of my jaw, neck or legs whenever I was about to fall asleep. Because their attack was more intense at night, I tried to sleep during the day.

Holy Communion and Unholy Terror

Those closing days of December 1970 were, indeed, dark. And early New Year's Morning 1971, I seemed to hit bottom. After receiving midnight communion at a watch night service, I was filled with absolute terror. Much like researchers with electronic probes, the demons within my body were able to activate fear and terror at will. I was in such distress I doubted my ability to safely drive my mother's car home, but I managed it. This illustrates an important point: My fear greatly exaggerated the demons' limited power of control over a Christian still able to resist them.

At home my elderly mother retired at once and I finally collapsed in despair on the patterned green linoleum floor of her modest living room. I knew the hideous, claustrophobic sensation of being trapped within my own body by the evil spirits. I feared demon control, but suicide and death seemed the only way out. Rejecting these ungodly ideas, I finally "kissed my chains" by accepting my miserable situation as the result of my own folly, trusting my life and salvation to God and letting go of the intolerable burden of constant resistance. This led to a respite after 4:00 am, but not to sleep.

Providentially, an announcer on KVIP, the recently established local Christian AM radio station, was reading through the entire New Testament to start the New Year. Listening to the Scriptures was comforting. Nevertheless, sleep, when it finally came in the afternoon, subjected me to a new level of demonic suppression of my mind, and I awoke completely disoriented and terrorized. My legs were kicking spontaneously and I felt again that I was facing demon control and death. Emotionally, this was the worst moment of my life, even more intense than the claustrophobic sense of being trapped in my own body that I felt only the night before, but mercifully of much shorter duration. For my mother put her hands on me and prayed, and I quickly regained control of my legs and comprehension of my situation.

Wrestling with the Evil Spirits

The spiritual struggle for the control of my body was being waged on three fronts: the emotional, the mental and the physical.

The most powerful attack was through fear: the terror that just welled up from within, the fear of falling under the control of the spirits and the fear of suicide and death.

The attack of the demons on my mind was both mental and physical: by day they injected evil thoughts and suggestions into my mind; by night or whenever I slept, they suppressed the brain, leaving me disoriented on awaking. The thoughts injected by day were blasphemous and obscene; the suggestions, murderous or suicidal. I recognized their satanic source and rejected all of them in the name of Jesus. Thus, the Lord gave me a way of escape from the options the demons had in mind for me: a mental ward, jail or death. But the spirits continued to press up through the nasal cavity and my mind was hindered by this pressure during the day, but sleep opened me up to even greater oppression so that sometimes I woke up in terror and without a sense of my relationship to God or consciousness of who or where I was.

The physical attacks included the palpable approach of the spirits outside trying to get into my body and the jerking of my muscles by the spirits already within. At first, the outsiders inspired terror by night, but they didn't persist for many nights. Apparently, they had to respect my continued rebukes in Jesus' name. The insiders, by contrast, hung on tenaciously and caused such physical weakness that back at school in Texas, for example, I suddenly found it difficult to climb a flight of stairs to the second floor of my dorm. My demons could alter my heartbeat and make the muscles in my body jerk or twitch, an ability that left the inside of my cheeks and the sides of my tongue cut up by my teeth because my jaws twitched sideways while I was chewing my food. Sometimes I bit my tongue hard, and I feared that it might be cut through during my violent sneezes. My tongue itself was distressing to look at in the mirror, not so much because of the many wounds along its sides as because, instead of resting quietly in my mouth, it seemed to have a life of its own rippling through it like a snake. This is a symptom of demonic occupation of the body I don't recall seeing mentioned elsewhere.

More subtle than the condition of my tongue but also distressing was the appearance of my eyes in the mirror: Perhaps it was only my imagination or a demonic suggestion, but I seemed to see something evil looking back at me. In addition, my hands were often painful or numb. Moreover, I had a characteristic light wheeze in breathing and speech. Headaches became more frequent later on as the spirits grudgingly began to leave.

Classic Symptoms of Demonization/Occupation

During this period, I had many of the classic symptoms of demonization: An afflatus (invisible but palpable spiritual presence) about the chest and solar plexus, twitching of muscles throughout the body, kinesis of pages of books while turning them and a slight kinesis of coins when handling them. Most annoyingly, the pages of my Bible followed and clung to my fingers as I turned their thin leaves. I twice observed and rebuked kinesis of physical objects in my mother's house: once in a dish balanced in the drying rack and once in an oriental wind chime. The wind chime hanging above me in the living room suddenly rang as a spirit apparently ascended into it directly from me. We tossed it out. My mother made light of the rocking dish, stopping its unusual motion with her hand after I angrily rebuked the spirits in the name of Jesus. Although I was outraged at the gall of these now unwelcome spirits, it was good that Mom could still take lightly such petty harassment in the midst of the battle we were in. Given my sharp rebuke and her lack of regard for the phenomenon, such gross kinesis never recurred.

Objects very near my body were harder to control; the kinesis of pages and coins under my touch persisted disturbingly for some time. Not then a student of demonology, I experienced many of these symptoms before I ever read or heard of them. The muscular twitches were an exception because I seem to recall Shakespeare's describing the twitches of a madman caused by his familiar spirits.

Thus, with evil spirits within and without my body, I spent the last days of 1970 and the first days of 1971 in seemingly dubious battle. Excerpts from my hand-written journal for those days and the next several months follow in Chapters 15 through 17.

"My heart is in anguish within me; the terrors of death assail me. Fear and trembling have beset me; horror has overwhelmed me"
(Psalm 55:4-5).

15

In Dubious Battle: Journal Excerpts, December 31, 1970, to January 13, 1971

When I realized that I might be in for an extended struggle against the evil spirits in my body, I began to record my experiences in a handwritten journal for the rest of that academic year. My journal began on the fourth day after consulting Pastor Smith, who had set me on the path of resistance to the deceiving spirits. Some of my interpretations of what the demons inside my body were doing were mistaken, but my basic account of internal and external events was accurate. My confusion is sometimes obvious, but this primary document preserves the details of the terrors I suffered and of the progress I made.

The introductions, the two long interpolations and the conclusions newly written for Chapters 15 through 17 are in italics. My short explanatory interpolations are in brackets. Most personal names have been changed to preserve privacy. This chapter covers the rest of the Christmas vacation that I spent at my mother's home in Redding, California.

December 31, 1970, Thursday, New Year's Eve Day

Went to bed at 4:00 pm [sic, should be am] without awakening mother. Demons loose [seeming to move about]. Awakened at 4:30 mind already confused, faith out of focus. When I awakened 2 hours later my mind was in much better shape. Mother's prayers necessary to a safe sleep.

On arising at 8:00, demons very tight before and behind, over shoulders. Prayer for clearing of mind first, but difficult. // // Double impulse into the brain. [The slashes and text following refer to a sensation *inside* the brain somewhat like that from being slapped on the head a couple of times.]

8:30 ff. [I'm] gaining ground through Christ's lifting of the coat of demonic mail upon me.

Took a bath--

9:25 Prayer to loosen [demonic] influence on body.

9:50 Reading in Revelation of a glorified Christ, Church of Laodicea. [I] felt demon influence begin to rise from skull.

10:05 Began to read, reread *The Spiritual Man* [v. 3, Nee]

4:00 pm. Intense shaking, commanded departure, lessening of demon influence. Pain in neck, resistance.

5:10 An assault, chill about the heart, chest.

5:35 Physical weakness a problem.

Fear and doubt and loss of certainty of physical control. . . . [A pastor's] prayer with me followed by increase of pressure on brain. . . . Suffering moderate awaiting communion [at watch night service], intense driving home and after arrival up to 4:00 am.

January 1, 1971, Friday, New Year's Day

Apparent defeat by the enemy cedes to respite, no sleep. Took a bath about 7:00 am. Finally lay down to sleep about 11 am. Worked out a plan of resistance after awakening at 12:15. Ate a bowl of soup and reread a chapter in the Nee work. Listened to KVIP [Christian radio] reading of the Word all day. Slept from 1:30-3:30 [pm] more or less. . . .

Dedicated myself to Jesus and set alarms to awaken hourly but of no avail. Forgot to pull alarm button for 1 pm. Attack upon me by demon lodged in back, neck. Loss of world orientation, fear. Then loss of control of legs, faced with death.

Mother helped by putting her hands on me and praying. Lucid comprehension of the situation followed. The demon in my back advanced on the brain via the neck and neck bone it occupies to frighten me with death and attack my faith.

They are bluffing, [but] they are difficult to control. . . .

7:30 pm. Hey, I'm stronger than they are and I can occupy more of my body than they can.

Incident of the Chinese bell [wind] chime [As I was praying and commanding demons to depart I coughed or sneezed and whatever left my body went up through the brass chime ringing it. I became upset at the idea of having a bell for demons in the house and Mother threw it outside.]

Couldn't get rid of them finally. Stayed up till about 4. Slept till 7:30~ with awakening between.

January 2, Saturday

Was the apparent power I had over them from the "pressure point" a lying wonder?

Awaken at 5 pm [am]. Again overslept (from 4 p [am]) because a live station not tuned [on radio]. . . .

Awaken at 7:15 am to KVCV? news.

Await KVIP, 7:30 [Christian station].

Reawaken at 8:00~ to the Word. Morning prayer, considerable fear, assailed by doubts. . .

9:00 am breakfast.

Demons tight. The one in shoulders not felt (at all). The front one keeping close. Question in my mind as to whether to leave resistance to the will of God passively or whether to actively oppose. Difficult because the demons very unresponsive to command. But finally about l0 or 11 he began to move out visibly. [That a visible effluvium was leaving my body may have been an illusion.] This provoked greater resistance from me while listening to the Word on KVIP. By 12:00 news confident of early victory. Began to read Ephesians (12:21 pm).

6:30 pm. Fear of loss of control, [demon] possession very great.

Here I used "possession" to mean the total control by demons that I so greatly feared and that they never attained. I was not "possessed" in that sense, but the demons within my body could trigger my emotions of fear and anxiety and cause my muscles to twitch or jerk. Now I prefer to avoid this term, and, instead, use "demonized" to include a continuum from the unnoticed presence of a demon within the body to complete control of a person by one or more demons. While I consider the term "demonized" superior to "possessed," I sometimes use the traditional term because it is still usual in English Bibles and in common speech.

Withstood attack by intercession breaking loose the back one as never before.

I talked to Erica [by telephone]. She said that they [*the demons*] are not to be feared. . . .

7:30 pm. Hey, I'm stronger than they are and I can occupy more of my body than they can.

Incident of the Chinese bell [wind] chime [As I was praying and commanding demons to depart I coughed or sneezed and whatever left my body went up through the brass chime ringing it. I became upset at the idea of having a bell for demons in the house and Mother threw it outside.]

Couldn't get rid of them finally. Stayed up till about 4. Slept till 7:30~ with awakening between.

January 13, Wednesday

Awakened at 5:15 am. Alerted myself with coffee and moving about. Prayed. Cooked breakfast at 7:30. Mother left and I spent some time in prayer and reading the book on the devil. Sharp pain in the throat made it difficult to swallow for a short time. No great progress in breaking the enemy loose physically, but some good moments of prayer and intercession. . . .

[My brother and I pull the head off a car engine] in the snow. . . . Feeling generally good, but considerable oppression and sleepiness in afternoon. Took a bath. . . .

Mother and I went to . . . a prayer meeting. I am under sharp assault (soft fluffy, seductive form) and my . . . [ordering the demons] is not too effective. On return home, I am under // // direct assault to the brain as I have not experienced for some time. Pressure in nose not exceptionally intense. I am not very apprehensive. Jesus brought me this far. He will have to bring me the rest of the way. Some difficulty reading [aloud] perfectly. While working on . . . [the] car I had a rather severe neck cramp and it appears that my neck and brain are real targets. . . .

"I will bear the indignation of the Lord because I have sinned against him, until he pleads my cause and executes judgment for me. He will bring me out to the light." (Micah 7:9a-b, ESV).

16

Surviving the Occupation: Journal Excerpts, January 14 to March 14, 1971

I can't compute the number of demons I had received over the 6 months from June through December, 1970, during which I was being deceived by them because I didn't know that they were demons and that I was really dealing with more than the first demon who had claimed to be Jesus. Nevertheless, they couldn't flood in at will. I believe that they entered my body one at a time as I, in effect, gave them permission by receiving them in my quasi-sexual experience of bridal mysticism.

Thus, in 6 months, I could have received 180 different spirits, but I really have no idea how many there were. That I survived occupation by many demons without coming under demonic control and descending into madness is a testimony to the truth of the Scripture that says, "The one who is in you is greater than the one who is in the world" (1 John 4:4b).

Getting rid of those spirits has been difficult and, surprisingly enough, I found that, in addition to spiritual means of grace, applying physical pressure to my body seemed to bring some relief. That is mainly why I sometimes slept on the hard floor or put notebooks under my spine and wore headbands. The headbands also seemed to relieve and limit the headaches I endured. My frequent high-pressure showers seemed to have similar effects.

Excerpts from my journal entries showing my struggles, victories, defeats, and gradual progress for the rest of January and the first half of March follow.

January 14, Thursday

Got up at 5:15 am and went to airport with Mother. Flight to SF not bad but the long layover at SF Airport was dismaying at first. I was afraid I couldn't make it. I gave the stewardess and the man at the American [Airlines] information counter a tract. Read in 1 Corinthians "and I would not that ye should have fellowship with devils" [KJV] (10:20). Gave another "Thank You" tract to the girl at the snack bar. . . .

We finally got off [the ground] at 12:45 pm. Under considerable physical oppression. The Lord gave me the opportunity to give the stewardess a "Thank You" card under favorable circumstances. Read Watchman Nee's *Release of the Spirit*. Gave my seat partner a tract on leaving and one to the sailor (Four Laws) in the terminal.

[On arriving in Dallas,] called Tim who was expecting me. . . .

January 20, Wednesday

I feel better, but with a sense of the deep penetration [by demons] to which I am subject. Seems to have deepened over last two days though the opposite may be true. After lunch I bought the Nietzsche collection and went over to the library until 3:30 pm. Talked to my pastor. Demon putting out false sweetness, good rays. Prof Y's class enjoyable, comprehensible. World beginning to come to life. Throwing it off the brain via nose seemingly. Becoming obtrusive about my belly. Bed at 11:30 pm. Good outlook. Beware the assault.

February 7, Sunday #41 [Day 41 of resistance]

Cloudy and quite cold—A GOOD DAY PTL.

I am much improved and have about overcome the dread and loneliness I have experienced every day until yesterday since I have been here and worse previously. Feelings, of course, don't fully reflect one's condition, but a person normally feels good. My physical strength is returning. I run to the glory of God to the cafeteria and back.

Sunday school class so, so. I was feeling a bit lonely on arrival . . . but the class was better. The Pastor's sermon was on the

"Invisible War, the War on the Saints." Text from 2 Timothy 2. He emphasized the militant nature of the conflict and the logical requirement of commitment to Jesus. He did not broach the topic of discernment of spirits. In the afternoon, I worked with Ephesians memorizing a couple of more verses and read successfully *Philoctetes*—a major accomplishment.

Wrote a letter to mother. . . . Ate dinner with Jon, Tim and Carl. I was greatly at ease waiting in line and eating as I have not been for some time. I rejoiced to go to church in the snow. . . . My pastor preached on the subject of Jeremiah 29:12-13. . . . Pastor advised people not to seek spiritual gifts nor an experience. Seek God, seek Jesus only, desperately.

Didn't get to sleep very well, thought life beginning to be [demonically] energized again. Got up at 1:00 am for honey and water. Joe dropped in so I offered him hot water for tea and a roll, showed him the night sky and read the passages from Hebrews and Colossians setting forth Christ the Creator and upholder of the universe. Went back to bed and slept till 2:30? when I awoke afraid and got up but immediately calmed. I went back to sleep until 6:00 when I had to go to the bathroom. . . .

February 21, Sunday

Morning service devoted to arranging the baptism of [church] members converted subsequent to original baptism. [*These church members getting saved was an indication of the impact of the revival we were in.*] I was late for lunch. . . .

February 23, Tuesday

I had breakfast with T. and R. . . . Left for Dallas Theological and Francis Schaeffer. Met Harold . . . but sat alone. Schaeffer quite good. Returned in time for lunch with [a professor]. We discussed Schaeffer et al.

I attempted to pray down my release but was discouraged and tempted to collapse. Refused and pulled up to do my working. . . .

Class not bad. . . . only a twinge of fear. No stupid remarks on my part. Talked with Professor afterwards. . . . Going to bed about 1:00 am.

Severe demonic assault. Left pretty groggy. Record player acting up. Records cut up.

March 11, Thursday

Bad night including nightmare I recall. After breakfast after brief reading of Romans 6, 8? I complete Book II of Rabelais before lunch. Returning from lunch I pray for a topic and immediately receive idea for paper on the two nonsense debates in Book II. The paper is written easily and completed by 3:30~. I do some light calisthenics upstairs and run a little. Meet Jill and tell her of the inspiration for my paper.

Dinner alone with Jesus. The *Baptist Standard's* reports of revival convicted me and I returned home to prostrate myself with tears before the Lord. Recover and go to class. Not bad but I begin to feel sickish and I leave at 8:40 break. Shower and go to Gene B's for the fellowship. Romans 6. These people understand the word. Return home and pray until 1:00 am. Bed in bed by heater, heat off. Pray for a good night's sleep. Some twitching of legs, surface phenomena (?), but I sleep soundly.

March 14, Sunday

Somewhat beaten down but OK at 8:00 am. Masaaki and Toshio go to church with me. They have difficulty understanding. Real gospel sermon from John. . . . Went to hear Jay P.'s testimony. No work today. Did return the book I had out. . . .

Summing up: I rarely bite my tongue now and the inside of my cheeks have healed indicating the degree to which I control the nerves and muscles of the jaw. Very obtrusive effluence by way of the nasal passages occurs at will while awake. Demons are becoming more obtrusive about the surface of my body, sneezing and effluence via the ears occurs several times daily. Some pain in body, hands, etc., but not as severe as previously and little of numbness. Little tingling in feet after kneeling, but spine is sometimes painful, still a center for occupation. My entire body is sensitive to pressure, e.g., the shower stream when concentrated causing an audible effluence via the nose. . . .

Bed on the floor tonight. 11:10 pm. Nightmare about entry into a monastery—I escaped. Good night's sleep. Awoke at 3:30 am~, 6:30.

"Oh that I had the wings of a dove! I would fly away and be at rest—I would flee far away and stay in the desert"
(Psalm 55:6-7).

17

I'm Not the Only One!
Journal Excerpts, March 17 to May 23, 1971

My condition was gradually improving as indicated by improved mood, improved jaw-muscle control and my getting some good nights of sleep; but I was still far from being back to normal. Although I was not under the constant severe anxiety of the early weeks of my ordeal, the last part of March was one of the worst periods since then. Conditions became so depressing that I was driven to seek a temporary respite at brother Joseph's home where, providentially enough, I learned that Satan was using a scam similar to that with which he had deceived me against someone else, his wife Lara.

March 17, Wednesday
Up at 8:10 am. . . .
Class a bit difficult with oppression of brain, speech centers. At home demons are obtrusive about the surface of the body. I witness to Masaaki telling him the gospel from the top (creation). I lose the train of my thought only once (par). Demons obtrusive about abdomen . . . as I retire. Awakened under assault, physical and mental (fear, doubt, despair) but mind clear though nose somewhat stopped up by mucus. Resisted on the power of the blood, rebuke, resistance to fear, etc., death in Christ. Forgot to turn on records for a while. Finally got to sleep with dreams. . . .

March 18, Thursday

Awakened by alarm at 8:10. Spent am in reading Matthew, RSV, and *War on the Saints*. Clarified basis of cross as freedom from guilt of sin, freedom from power of sin, freedom from power of Satan. Finally got to prayers for lost, the brethren at noon. . . . Wrote up these notes (2 p). Finished reading *Midsummer Nights Dream* with God's help by 4:00 pm. Twenty set ups, 10 pushups, 4 leg lifts, 20 toe touches. . . . Run only one lap . . . wind[y]. . . .

March 23, Tuesday

Massaged head a little to begin effluence and got up to shower. . . . God is faithful. I bit my cheek on the left side at breakfast, but my jaw control is much better. Only biting the side of my tongue rarely and so far today not at all at the tip. 9:15. . . .

Prepared for Nietzsche class with a shower, dressed in blue trousers, gold tie that Chumphot just gave me. No good. I am under terrible assault in class, so I leave in less than an hour. Asked Jill to drive me over to Brother Joseph's so I used her phone to call up Lara. Feel better almost immediately. Let Jill go and took a shower before driving over to Joseph's.

Over there, Joseph is a bit taken aback by my condition, but they put me up OK. Ken's room [is a] bit of a mess. I slept according to usual pattern awaking once one-half to one hour after retiring, second at 5:30 am. Slept in until about 7:00 so as not to disturb anyone.

March 24, Wednesday

Got up and Lara told me of a recent experience. She had been praying to the Holy Spirit to live her life for her when she was approached by a dark spiritual presence. She rejected it as she felt herself "going under" because she recognized that it was not of the Lord.

Lara's experience well illustrates Jessie Penn-Lewis's analysis in War on the Saints *of what can make believers vulnerable to demonic incursion. Penn-Lewis says that mis-location of the God to whom we pray ("Our Father in heaven", ESV) from up in heaven to down on earth can be dangerous. Even more risky is a passivity that mistakenly expects God to directly impel us to action instead of gently inviting us to think, will and act in obedience to his word and Spirit*

Thus, Lara may have been praying to the Holy Spirit within or about her. This may invite demonic intervention. And in asking the Holy Spirit to "live her life for her," Lara may have been asking for God to make things easier by directly controlling her actions instead of by enlisting her willing cooperation. But the dark spirit whose presence she sensed was ready to take control of her life in just that way. Fortunately, Lara recognized the counterfeit before "going under" its control.

April 8, Thursday

Up at 7:15. Shower until 8:30. Breakfast with the Korean girls. Christian testimony.

100 days resistance.

AM spent in prayer, reading first four chapters in John in Williams translation and studying the witness plan. Lunch with Maasaki. Discussion of universality of Christianity. Attempt to float witness plan aborted, but a cordial discussion of the claims of Christianity. . . .

20 setups, 3 leg overs, 3 leg lifts, 10 pushups, 10 touch toes.

Met D. after run and told him to teach English to his foreign students so I could preach them the gospel. Gave him a Four Spiritual Laws tract to illustrate what I wanted them to understand verbally. Called up Toshio. He is in a cancer hospital. Serious? . . .

Good [prayer group] meeting. We prayed twice, once for guidance. Read I Corinthians 13. Love in the Christian life. Prayer for the lost friends, relatives. Everyone in agreement, problem of predestination opened.

Shower and bed at 1:30-2:00 am. . . . Turned head of bed. Good sleep. Don't recall awakening before light.

April 9, Good Friday

Up at 8:15. Head not in bad shape. Shower.

Impressed by the Spirit (Holy) to go to Pancake House for breakfast. Tremendous line there, but I resisted impulse to leave and a salesman came in and sat down beside me. He asked if I was a Jehovah's Witness because I was reading a Baptist Standard. I got the opportunity to witness for Jesus, of course.

Picked up a copy of the Sermon on the Mount in Japanese/English. . . . Maasaki suggested we go to the Christian Arts Festival. Saw the "Long Road Back" on the Jesus People. . . . Found Maasaki a Japanese/English Bible. Praise the Lord. . . . Called the Vs. for prayer for my oriental friends. . . .

Demons giving me some muscular twitches in legs. Gave me some uneasiness at being without a release of pressure in head by massage or shower for so long downtown. 11:30. Shower, bed on floor. 12:45 am prayer.

Awoke in some fear. Set records going and went back to bed.

April 11, Easter Sunday
Usual Sunday am dumps. Up at 8:30 am. Mr. Li not up. Car broke down. Fan belt stolen. Mike gave me a ride to town. Great sermon by brother D. on the resurrection. Joseph had me give the opening prayer in class. Sharp discussion over the assurance of salvation.

Jim gave me a ride home as expected of the Lord. . . .

April 14, Wednesday
Difficulties. . . .Went through the Spirit filled life tract and was assaulted by loving sensation I assume not from the Lord. Resisted, prayed. OK. My body is thoroughly permeated by demon(s). They are being thrown off only gradually.

Prof. Y's class not bad, but pressure built up so that I took four showers during day. AM → midnight.

Witnessing class OK. Slept in bed, awakened once or twice.

April 15, Thursday
Up at 7:30. Shower. Read from Hebrews as depression over occupation of body grew. Prayed to Jesus to help me with paper. He helped. I'm finished at 11 am. . . . Very difficult to stay awake. Prayed for quickening power, but still sleepy. Ran track. . . .

Brief evening [academic] class. Arrived at Blaylocks' in time for witnessing class. Returned home and showered, prayed, wrote this up, bed at 1:00 pm—*Bad night, physical assault of twitching*— (Idea of leading Toshio to the Lord.)

April 16, Friday
Got up at 6:30 am~ to be ready to take Toshio to Samuell Clinic. Did it. He suggested I not wait but I waited. On return I

asked him if he had thought about spiritual things while in the hospital and he had thought about death. I invited him to my room and explained the plan of salvation according to our witnessing class procedure. He was hesitant but was finally able to repeat the sinner's prayer after me.

Took P. to SMU. Called up for a Bible for Toshio and received the offer of a good one, bilingual, from the Gideon man.

Took Toshio to prayer and Bible study at Daniels'. Tried to get him to pray with me but he was unable to speak.

April 24, Saturday

Up at 7 am, brief shower, over to prayer breakfast. Helped me though had a coughing fit at close of prayer. Distributed anti-Satan tract. Returned home, read Romans ?, I Corinthians. . . . Took a run at 2:30~ over half way around football field.

Change in condition. Head under much less pressure today. Effluence is springing from throat via floor of mouth more than from spine/head? Still severe cough though perhaps less than yesterday.

Not a bad night.

May 2, Sunday

Awakened at 7 am, got up by 7:45.

Good discussion in class. T. on wrong end but less aggressive. Brother D. inspired. Sermon on the power, straitness of the gospel.

Afternoon spent in reading Wimsatt, laundry, Jae Soo's Bible study. James Robison very powerful. Went to T.'s by mistake, but welcomed as a brother. . . .

Effluence from throat, floor of mouth. Afflatus prominent, not as obtrusive as a month ago. 12:45 am.

May 12, Wednesday

Typed up paper for Prof. Y on Wimsatt's book in morning. . . . Got exam from Prof. Y, talked to P. about Donald Davidson, borrowed *Still Rebels, Still Yankees* from A. G.

Went to church. Ron Dunn zeroed in perfectly on Satan. Good testimonies. Steve, Gene sang, testified.

Sleeping in bed without light. Awoke at 3:30. . . . Left light on again.

May 21, Friday

Up about 7:30-8:00~ am. Shower. Breakfast at snack bar. Morning at library.

Afternoon, shower, went to get clothes, to get tapes, to get dinner. Read in Luke. Demons somewhat obtrusive. Afflatus on chest about back. Twitching in legs, slight tendency toward numbness.

Slept on floor. Tape of sermon on "Being Filled with the Spirit." Cough in morning.

May 23, Sunday

Awaken about 8 am. Shower 8-9~ am. Breakfast at Ramada— Calm in chaos. They were a mess. Sunday school, Karl's testimony. Rapid effluence without coughing, discomfort.

Prayed for the graduating class at . . . graduation (individually). Rested until 5:00 pm. Ate at Dairy Queen.

Pastor's class, ordination service. . . .

[Listened to] Billy Graham, Radio Bible Class, Back to Bible, etc. Shower. To bed on floor complete with tape on filling with the Spirit. Awakened at 3:30 am.

Dream including someone preaching against Satan which is understandable since I've been listening to such a sermon on tape. Cat came in the door which was open. Got up, turned over tape. Awoke again at 7:00 am

This concludes the excerpts from my journal for the most intense period of my restoration with its confusion, emotional suffering and physical pain and discomfort along with my gradual increase in physical and spiritual strength. I would gladly have accepted much more help than was then available from the church, but restoration from this kind of affliction will require that the occupied or demonized person learn to "be strong in the Lord and in his mighty power." And he or she may sometimes have to stand alone with the Lord.

In the next chapter, I present the indications of demonization along with possible causes for it.

"Beloved, do not believe every spirit, but test the spirits to see whether they are from God, for many false prophets have gone out into the world" (1 John 4:1, ESV).

18

Indications and Causes of Demonization

Indications of Demonization

Now, the biblical truth that a Christian can be demonized, that is, occupied and controlled by demons to a greater or lesser extent, offers hope—but no excuses—for Christians whose sins have given demons entrance into their bodies. The question remains for the believer experiencing any affliction that could be caused by demons, "Have I become demonized?" In most cases, the presence of evil spirits can be determined from the five spiritual indications of demonization that follow. Given a positive determination, the source or cause can then be traced either to sins and practices in the believer's life or to heritages known to lead to demonization.

Five indications of the presence and activity of demons are

1. Hatred, hostility and outbursts of anger or violence
2. Fear and anxiety resulting from any spiritual practice or experience
3. Obedience to false guidance thought to be from God but in reality from evil spirits
4. Passivity of mind, emotions, will or body during any spiritual experience

5. Supernatural physical manifestations that appeal to the senses and to pride

These five indications are discussed in the following five paragraphs.

First, hatred, hostility, rage and outbursts of anger or violence strongly suggest demonization. Indeed, Ephesians 4:29 implies that unresolved anger can "give the devil a foothold."

Second, fear that springs not from a righteous awe of holy God, or a present danger but from an unknown cause following on doubtful spiritual practices suggests the presence of demons. For as Paul writes in Romans 8:15, "You did not receive a spirit that makes you a slave again to fear, but you received the Spirit of sonship. And by him we cry, 'Abba, Father.'"

Third, all human beings including Christians are subject to the injection of demonic ideas and suggestions into their minds. Therefore, this in itself is not a symptom of demonization. Demon-injected ideas can be recognized by their abrupt appearance fully formed and unrelated to the natural working of the mind. Their driving energy and obsessive persistence are also characteristic. Their content may be obviously evil or may appear to be spiritual guidance from God. When their content is not obviously evil, the satanic source of these ideas can still be recognized by their just-described characteristics. Their evil source should be rebuked just as Jesus did in the temptation (Matt. 4:1-11). *But if, instead, a Christian believes and obeys such demonic lies, he will become demonized.* Therefore, habitual acceptance of and obedience to this kind of false spiritual guidance is both a cause and an indication of demonization.

Fourth, passivity in any area of life may be indicative of demon incursion because demons seek to displace the human mind and will from their rightful control of body and soul. Such *passivity* is defined as *a person's abandonment of his normal, God-given control of any of his faculties of body or mind.* And passivity is the necessary and sufficient condition for demon activity in human beings. If you have practiced any of the meditative techniques of Eastern religion—and of some forms of Christian mysticism—to the empty-minded or "centered" state, you have experienced undue passivity and may have received demons into your body. This may also occur if a Christian abdicates his responsibility to actively think and act in obedience to the promptings of the Holy Spirit. Submission to the Holy Spirit requires active engagement of the believer's faculties. Christians who expect the Holy Spirit to think for them and to impose His will mechanically will, instead, find themselves controlled mentally and physically by unholy spirits.

Fifth, physical or sensate supernatural manifestations suggest an advanced state of demonic activity and demonization. These manifestations are supernatural and spiritual in that they are produced by evil spirits, but they appeal not to the regenerated human spirit, but to the sinful flesh through the senses and through pride.

Presence of any of these five indications suggests the presence of demons. In addition, confusion is often seen in the demonized along with any of the other indications.

Multiple Causes of Mental and Emotional Affliction

Conditions such as depression can come from experiential, relational, physiological, genetic or psychological causes; and such conditions should be distinguished from symptoms of demonization by determining the underlying causes of affliction. Consultation with medical professionals in these fields may be necessary to sort such matters out. In *The Handbook for Spiritual Warfare*, Dr. Ed Murphy warns against treating every condition that resembles demonization as demonic. If, for example, you have a chemical imbalance that affects the brain, you may need medication to maintain normal brain chemistry and there should be neither denial of such necessity nor any stigma from it.

The matter is further complicated because Satan is no gentleman; he will readily pile demonic affliction upon persons with physical or psychological afflictions if he has been given access through heritage, abuse in childhood, occult involvement or any other basis for demonic incursion. In *Demon Possession & the Christian*, C. Fred Dickason shows how medical and spiritual counselors can cooperate in the healing of a person with both natural and supernatural causes of an affliction.

The Doors for Demons

The most common causes of demonization in today's American culture are probably unforgiveness, sexual sin, drug use (biblical *pharmakeía*), occultism and false (non-Christian) religions. In Chapter 54 of his handbook, Dr. Murphy discusses six sin areas that may cause demonization: generational sin (family heritage); abuse in childhood; social sins (e.g., hatred, bitterness, rebellion): sexual sin; satanic curses; and occult practices. Neil T. Anderson's *The Bondage Breaker* includes an appendix titled "Non-Christian Spiritual Experience Inventory" with lists for Occult, Cults and Other Religions. My Annotated Bibliography lists other books dealing with the many possible causes of demonization. These references may be helpful if the underlying cause of demonization is not obvious. In the rest of this chapter, I cite some counterfeits demons use to deceive and demonize believers. In addition, I discuss some spiritual and therapeutic practices that Christians today are using without understanding their dangers.

Spiritual Counterfeits

All Christians need to learn how to distinguish evil spirits from the Holy Spirit to avoid counterfeit spiritual experiences. First, simply obey the commands of Scripture so that your spirit is not dulled by the effects of sin. Rigorous obedience to the commands of Ephesians 5:18-19 to "be being filled with the Spirit, speaking to yourselves with psalms, hymns and spiritual songs, singing and praising in your heart to the Lord," in itself, would be sufficient (my translation). But when one fails in sensitivity and obedience to the Holy Spirit as I did, other means of discernment may still save you from demonization. Therefore, it is important to understand the ploys Satan uses to deceive believers: The lie injected into the mind as already discussed will normally accompany 1) Supernatural physical manifestations of all kinds including counterfeit gifts of the Holy Spirit or 2) Impersonations, visible or invisible, of human beings, of angels or of God.

Spiritual counterfeits of the things of God are used by Satan as bait to mislead the spiritual Christian who seeks God and rejects the lusts of the flesh and of the mind. Demons may manifest themselves to the senses of believers in different ways simultaneously with mental suggestions tailored to the targeted Christian. Demons commonly claim to be a departed loved one, a holy angel or a person of the Trinity. They may offer counterfeit spiritual gifts, imitations of divine love or the guidance that some

Christians seek in the wrong way, i.e., passively. Such gifts and guidance require the suppression of the believers mind and will to a state of passive or mechanical obedience to the "divine revelations." The demons' goal is a complete passivity of the believer's mind, will, emotions and body such that the demons are free to control the person through the nervous system.

Such supernatural manifestations are not usually offered to Christians seduced by the individualism and materialism of American life because such Christians pose no threat to Satan's world system. But as soon as a Christian arouses himself to diligently seek the Lord, Satan may counterattack with his counterfeits. If the awakened Christian is misled into accepting some false spiritual manifestation or demonic guidance, he may continue for some time doing good work for God on the one hand while being led away from God, perhaps into a cult, on the other. Sooner or later either the Christian will be rendered useless to the kingdom of God or he will become aware that something is terribly wrong in his spiritual experience. In *War on the Saints*, Jessie Penn-Lewis points out how the spirits who at first puffed the believer up with physical manifestations that made him believe he was a special object of God's love and favor may later inflict such intense emotional and physical suffering on him that he despairs of life. The demons may then tell their victim the lie that his suffering is from and for God. He desperately needs to learn the truth that his suffering is caused not by God, but by Satan. The previously listed indications of demonization will probably reveal a demonic source for such suffering.

Yoga and Other Mysticisms

I would caution Christian readers that hatha yoga is not an exercise regime or a physical therapy, but an integral part of an ancient spiritual discipline. Indeed, "yoga" is the Sanskrit word for "yoking" and refers to union with the "god" within. So all eight forms of yoga have the same goal of inducing and enhancing the unitive mystical experience that has convinced the yogis and their followers of their own divinity. But the Scriptures teach that humans are not God but fallen creatures of God whose redemption required Jesus Christ to die on a Roman cross for our sins. Indeed, to confuse the creature, man, with the Creator is a New Testament definition of idolatry (Romans 1:25). Therefore, those who by accident or design attain to the real goal of yoga, the illusion of their union with God, may be deceived into violating the Second Commandment, which forbids idolatry. And even if they avoid this snare, Christians who appropriate this alien spiritual discipline for their physical well being may encounter demons while passively holding still in their *asanas* (yoga positions).

If you have tried hatha yoga and found that it relieved back pain, for example, I still suggest that you seek out one of the many therapeutic regimes *completely divorced* from any Pagan religious system. Even then, you must discern whether the exercises or positions are having psycho-physiological effects that tend to put your mind into the passive or "centered" state. Avoid any practice that does this. Ask God to show you safe ways to wisely deal with your condition without risking demonic incursion.

Furthermore, Christians who mix yogic meditation with their prayers are misguided. The preliminary goal of Eastern meditation is the "centered" mind emptied of thought. This is the antithesis of Christian meditation on the word or logos of God by means of which the actively engaged mind leads one to deeper personal knowledge of the eternal logos of God, Jesus Christ. Indeed, the "centered" or empty mind is the mental state sought by mediums and channelers to receive revelations from their familiar spirits. Christians who practice mental passivity by means of either the physical or the mental disciplines of yoga will encounter demons, because passivity is the *necessary and sufficient condition* for demonic activity in human beings. Indeed, some Christian mystical traditions such as those of Pseudo-Dionysius and *The Cloud of Unknowing* may also lead to passivity with the same predictable consequence of demonization. (See also Appendix A, pp. 129-30.)

Ayurveda

While the occultic healing systems of the East such as Ayurveda may well bear some valuable knowledge of herbal remedies, these systems are also fraught with spiritual (and physical) dangers. Their philosophies parallel that of yoga and are therefore spiritually misleading. Indeed, their practitioners may transmit evil spirits directly by means of their touch. I suspect that the Christian who submits to a physical manipulation by a New-

Age or Hindu healer, for example, may suffer demonic affliction because the practitioner may directly transmit one or more of her familiar spirits to the person under treatment. On the physical side, *Wikepedia* reports that studies of Ayurvedic herbs prepared in India show that some are contaminated with heavy metals.

Take your health problems to God for his healing and for his direction on other treatments that do not violate Scriptural principles. If you value Christ's approval more than your own comfort, you will prefer to forgo any treatment or practice based on an anti-Christian philosophy. Instead, you are free to approach the throne of grace for yourself or to request the prayers of the elders and saints (Ephesians 3:12, James 5:14-15).

Hypnotherapy

In Chapter 8 I tell of how my intuitive fear of demons spoiled my attempts to induce self-hypnosis with a recording. Although I was backslidden, I believe that the Holy Spirit was protecting me from another possible avenue of demonization because the hypnotic state is a passive state open to the suggestions of another consciousness, that of the hypnotist. Whether the hypnotist is a well-meaning but spiritually naïve Christian or a secularist psychologist, they have no right to meddle with your soul (psyche) at this level. And since this is yet another way to enter a state of mental passivity, you should not submit your mind to theirs. Your wakeful mind is the guardian of your soul and body; don't drop your conscious self-control (a fruit of the Spirit) except in normal sleep.

Books on Spiritual Warfare

When my battle began in 1970, I did well to find in Baptist circles one older pastor who correctly diagnosed my problem as demonic and gave me a copy of the Third Volume of Watchman Nee's *The Spiritual Man* to work through. Although I do not recommend this book overall, Volume 3 is still a useful reference for the demonized, especially for those who sense that their thinking abilities have gradually declined for no medical reason. Nee affirms that demons can induce in believers a gradual loss of the ability to concentrate and to control their thoughts. Such distraction and mental passivity were not problems for me, at least, not until the deceiving spirits turned on me, but Nee's recommendations for taking back control of the mind and body were still helpful.

Jessie Penn-Lewis's *War on the Saints* is the definitive work on the variety of spiritual counterfeits used by evil spirits to deceive believers. She also warns against the passivity that permits demons to gain control of the minds and bodies of believers.

Dr. Ed Murphy's *The Handbook for Spiritual Warfare* is a valuable guide to spiritual warfare. While providing practical guidance for expelling demons from the truly demonized, he recognizes that psychological conditions such as schizophrenia and depression may not involve demons at all. He further warns against confusing the personality segments or "alters" of those suffering from multiple personality disorder (MPD, DSM-II) with demons and forbids trying to expel the alters. Instead, he shows how the gospel provides the means to fuse the multiple personalities through bringing each to faith in Christ. C. Fred Dickason points out, however, that demonization by multiple demons is more common than MPD. [According to Wikepedia, American Psychiatric Association's *Diagnostic and Statistical Manual of Mental Disorders* (DSM) *IV-TR* now calls MPD dissociative identity disorder (DID)].

These books on demonology and others listed in the Annotated Bibliography make the point that the passivity of mind and body cultivated in New-Age, Buddhist and Hindu practices opens one up to evil spirits and has no place in Christian faith. These practices include various forms of yoga, meditation on (repetition of) a mantra, concentration of one's gaze on a mandala and concentration of the mind on one's own breath. "Christian Yoga," then, is an oxymoron; the two systems are antithetical.

The Next Step

Once a determination of demonization has been made and the sins or combination of heritage, sins, practices or experiences that gave rise to it have been discovered; the question becomes, "How do we get rid of the demons?" Practical answers drawn from the Scriptures and from my experience will be found in the next chapter, "The Means of Resistance and Victory."

"'So do not fear, for I am with you; do not be dismayed, for I am your God. I will strengthen you and help you; I will uphold you with my righteous right hand'" (Isaiah 41:10).

19

The Means of Resistance and Victory

Many demonized Christians may be able to oust their demons quickly by affirming their identity in Christ and using the authority of the name of Jesus. But God may graciously require some to seek prayer for deliverance from their churches and to be accountable to a brother or sister on the sins that let the demons in. And if one has been deceived by lies and false experiences for months or years, his deliverance may be gradual.

For those seeking guidance to victory over demonic affliction, I offer my personal counsel in the following brief section. In the rest of the chapter, I present an orderly listing of the means of resistance that I used against my demons. I am confident that believers who have submitted themselves to God in seeking victory over the devil will be able here to find for themselves what will be helpful in their battles. In addition, you may find in my account a kind of companion in suffering, in perseverance and in victory. The Psalmist, who, for example, concludes Psalm 40 with both an affirmation of faith and a cry for help, is another fellow sufferer with whom you can fellowship across the centuries. But finally, it is to the living Christ, who said, "Never will I leave you; never will I forsake you," *that you must look for full understanding and for strength.*

Preparation for the Battle

First Seek God's Guidance

If you found that you have some of the indications of demonization listed in the previous chapter, thank God for the light that he has given you. If you conclude from them that you have received demons into your life, consider the sins, the sin areas and the counterfeits mentioned in previous chapters for clues as to what may have given them entrance. If you are still not sure what led to your demonization, ask God to reveal to you the doorway(s) they used.

Confess and forsake all sins, lies, passivities and demonic manifestations when they are revealed. Confess your acceptance of false experiences and false manifestations as sinful intercourse with the Enemy, indeed, as idolatry. Ask God to forgive you and freely receive your forgiveness on the basis of God's promise that "if we confess our sins, he is faithful and just and will forgive us our sins and purify us from all unrighteousness" (1 John 1:9).

Renounce all lies and false experiences foisted on you by evil spirits by saying, "In the name of Jesus Christ, I reject every lie and I renounce every manifestation and false experience that I ever received from evil spirits." Be as specific as you can in naming the lies, manifestations and false experiences. Continue to reject the lies and renounce the experiences in the name of Jesus as they are revealed to you.

Christians suffering from demonic physical or mental afflictions should beware of the lie that these afflictions are from God and should be accepted. Discernment here is crucial.

Marshal the Artillery

Next read Revelation 12:10-12 and Philippians 2:5-11. Memorize Revelation 12:11 and personalize it in combination with Philippians 2:11 by saying: *"I testify to the overcoming power of the blood of the Lamb and of the word of my testimony that Jesus Christ is Lord to the glory of God the Father."* You will quickly learn this Scripture-based testimony as you wield it against the attacks of the evil spirits, which may become more intense before they begin to subside. For if you are demonized and you follow the light God has given you, your perseverance may be tested as things seem to get worse before they get better. *Nevertheless, if you are a believer, the Enemy cannot harm you as long as you keep your will set against him, reject his lies and refuse his seductive supernatural experiences*

Read Romans 6:1-14 until you grasp its teaching that Christ's death to sin has been credited to you by God and frees you from the power of sin. Personalize verse 11 by naming your sins as you say, for example, "*I count myself dead to cocaine (*or *witchcraft,* or *fornication,* etc.) *but alive to God in Christ Jesus.*"

You must take back the "foothold" or "place" (Greek *tópos,* Ephesians 4:27) you gave evil spirits to operate in your body and life by habitual sin, by believing their lies or by accepting their false spiritual experiences. The point is to take back the permission you once gave them by now *renouncing* your sins, *rejecting* their lies and *refusing* to receive their manifestations.

By verbal renunciation you set your will against what you previously accepted and you thus "resist the devil" so that "he will flee from you" as promised in James 4:7. How long must you continue active resistance? Until he flees, which, as noted previously, may take some time.

You should seek counsel beginning with a pastor or counselor in your church. If he doesn't understand your condition as you do, he can still pray for you. You may be able to find a more understanding counselor elsewhere, but a difference about just where the demons afflicting you are located or even whether demons are your problem is not a good reason to leave a church where you have encouraging fellowship. But if the pastor insists that you accept his theology that your body can't be occupied by a demon to fellowship in the church, and you are convinced otherwise; then you must stand by your conviction and leave.

You should also seek to be a part of a small relational group where people can pray for you and your afflictions even if they don't understand your condition. And don't hesitate to pray for others because your affliction doesn't disqualify you from the promise that through faith in our Lord Jesus Christ, "we may approach God with freedom and confidence" (Ephesians 3:11-12).

A Successful Campaign: The Means of Resistance

Returning to the account of my personal battle, I offer in the rest of this chapter the means of resisting the devil I found most helpful. Remember that life in this fallen world is no beach, but a brutal battleground against a bitter and ruthless enemy. "Therefore, since Christ suffered for us in the flesh, arm yourselves with the same mind" (1Peter 4:1a, NKJV).

Back in 1971, with evil spirits without and within my body, the battle seemed to me unequal, as it surely was except that God was on my side and his Holy Spirit was within me. Against the fear, the anxiety, the evil thoughts, the accusations, the confusion, the physical harassment and the physical pressure on my brain inflicted by the demons; I had many means of grace: Faith in Christ, confession and repentance for my sin, praise, prayer, fellowship, the word of God, the authority of Jesus' name, the righteousness of Christ and the power of Jesus' blood. In addition, I discovered some physical means that were helpful in the long battle that followed.

The spiritual means of resistance to the spirits that occupied my body began with confession and repentance for my sin and coming to a reassurance of salvation. The first step was to recognize that I had given myself over to evil spirits. I confessed, repented of and renounced in the name of Jesus my sin of idolatry, indeed, of spiritual adultery. In my confusion, I also had to discern whether or not I was a Christian, but my recent experience of re-conversion to Christ and the biblical basis of my trust in Christ alone for salvation were clear and I could find nothing more to commit to him. Those uncertain of their salvation should meditate on the biblical definition of saving faith of Romans 10:9: "If you confess with your mouth that Jesus is Lord and believe in your heart that God raised him from the dead, you will be saved" (ESV). Consider also 1 John 5:1-13, especially, verse 10.

Unpardonable Sin, Anyone?

Fortunately, I had been taught as a child that if you were afraid that you had committed the unpardonable sin, you could be sure that you hadn't. This still made such good sense to me that, despite his best efforts, the devil was unable to afflict me with that shopworn but scary accusation. The gist of the argument is that having committed the unpardonable sin is evidence of a conscience so hardened to the Spirit of God that such a person is no longer capable of having any concern for sin. Thus, anyone who shows enough concern for any sin to worry about its spiritual consequences cannot have sinned unpardonably. And Christ himself promises that "whoever comes to me I will never drive away" (John 6:37b). Remember these truths because demons are sure to use this false accusation to discourage the believer as soon as he realizes that he has sinned seriously and begins to repent.

The Word as Sword of the Spirit

Soon after I came back into fellowship with Christ in May, I had learned to recognize most satanic thoughts when spiritually injected into my mind. (Obviously, I missed the one in which the demon claimed to be "Jesus.") So usually I instantly responded to such thoughts with Christ's rebuke to Satan in the desert, "'Get thee hence, Satan, for it is written, "Thou shalt worship the Lord thy God and him only shalt thou serve"'" (Matthew 4:10). I also used other Scriptures as appropriate or just rebuked Satan in the name of Jesus. I believe that this means of God's grace protected me from complete confusion and demonic control even before I recognized my condition.

Orientation for Victory

First, those afflicted and those counseling the afflicted need to pray for discernment of the sins of the flesh that are at the root of any demon affliction (James 1:5). And don't neglect the possible influence of the sins of previous generations. The following checklist may be helpful in orienting the demonized for resistance to and victory over the devil:

1. Confess to God each of the sins that subjected you to demon affliction. They may include lust, greed, anger, unforgiveness, occultism, false religion, atheism, alcohol and drug use, and the sins of ancestors. Humble yourself completely by using plain language and being specific, honest and unsparing of yourself.

2. Thank God for forgiving you in accord with his promise of 1 John 1:9 and for Jesus' death for your sins on which all forgiveness depends.

3. Renounce the sins confessed in the name of Jesus. This sets your will against sin and Satan (1 Peter 5:8-9).

4. Command the spirits associated with the sins confessed to depart, e.g., "In the name of Jesus, I command the spirits of cocaine to get out of me" (James 4:7).

5. By God's grace, forgive anyone you can remember who has ever wronged you (Mark 11:25). For if you want to be freed from demonization, you simply must give up any grudges against those who have abused you and receive Christ's cleansing from all resentment, bitterness and hatred. (See Romans 12:19-21.)

Morning Reorientation: The Word as Balm and Bread

In the morning when I woke up, my mind was usually disoriented by the work of evil spirits during my sleep. So every morning, I prayed a prayer of commitment to Christ as Lord and proclaimed my resistance to Satan, among other things. I kept a written set of spiritual exercises I read every morning to get my head together, to reestablish conscious contact with the Lord and to resist the enemy by affirmations of my place in Christ and rebuke of the spirits. Some affirmations of the Christian's present inheritance in Christ are found in Ephesians 1:3-14, 2:13-22; Colossians 1:9-14; Romans 8:15-17. Affirmations of victory and authority over the devil are found in 1 John 3:8b, 4:4; Luke 10:17-20. Memorize and speak affirmations drawn from these or other Scriptures as the Spirit leads. See also the personalized scriptural affirmations under the next heading.

For about a year and a half, I spent most of my mornings reading the Bible to build myself up spiritually and to clear my mind for academic work in the afternoon. Only by spending much of my day in the Scriptures and prayer was I able to accomplish the study and writing demanded by my rigorous graduate program. At no time in my life have I lived more in accord with Paul's exhortation to "pray without ceasing."

The Authority of the Name, the Power of the Blood and the Power of the Word

I also began to exercise the authority of the name of Jesus directly against the presence of the spirits—with mixed results. The spirits outside gave ground early on if not immediately. But those already in my body were more stubborn, probably because I had willingly received them. For some time, I repetitiously commanded the spirits within to depart, but they didn't seem to budge for a long time. I now laugh to think of the spectacle of my obsessively—and ineffectively—ordering out the very spirits I had so recently welcomed in.

But it was no joke at the time as I suffered excruciating anxiety during the day and worse terrors at night. To help me stand against the terror from within, I took up a testimony based on Revelation 12:11, suggested by Derek Prince. I memorized and recited the entire verse, of course, but I also personalized it as Prince suggested by saying aloud, *"I testify to the overcoming power of the blood of the Lamb."* When I was exhausted, overwhelmed by fear, at the limit of my endurance and felt I could bear no more without losing control or going insane; God always honored that testimony with strength, a respite or sleep. The blood represents the death of Jesus for our sins that frees us from the power of sin and Satan. I don't think I even understood this basis of the power of the blood then, but it worked anyway. Such is the power of God's holy and enduring word.

I now prefer this *aggressive*, personalized combination of Revelation 12:11 and Philippians 2:11. *"I overcome you, Satan, by the blood of the lamb and by the word of my testimony that Jesus Christ is Lord, to the glory of God the Father."*

Praise and Music

The nights were always the worst; not for nothing did Jesus speak of "your hour and the power of darkness" on the night he was seized (Luke 22:53). Demonic nightmares, of course, were frequent and frightful. And at night the sleep, so necessary for strength to continue the struggle by day, made conscious resistance impossible and subjected me to such mental oppression that sometimes I awoke completely disoriented. By God's grace, these episodes were short and didn't persist beyond the early stages of the battle.

When I went to bed, I played long playing, microgroove records of traditional hymns on my phonograph to help me sleep with less oppression, but sometimes the music was disrupted when the light-weight pickup holding the phonograph needle skipped all the way across the record. Given the no-holds-barred battle I was in, I have no doubt that the skipping was caused by demonic kinesis. Modern

CD players are probably more resistant to such kinesis, but you still may have to rebuke the demons from your electronic devices.

In 1970-71, because of the move of the Holy Spirit across the land called the Jesus Movement, "Amazing Grace" was at or near the top of the charts of popular music for many months, with recordings by various popular artists including Joan Baez. Hearing that classic hymn in unexpected places always struck me as pure grace, filled me with gratitude and gave me a spiritual lift.

Then, I was not a strong singer, but one of the most powerful weapons against fear is to sing praises to God and songs about the blood or name of Jesus such as "There Is Power in the Blood" and "In the Name of Jesus." Since I learned to play the guitar to accompany my singing, this has become my preferred means to wield the power of Christ against fear and panic attacks. This point cannot be overemphasized. So if you are truly unable to sing, you should read or recite songs, traditional hymns and the psalms of praise from the Scriptures. God honors our heartfelt praises even if they lack the beauty of the voice of a talented singer.

A strategic time for praise is just before you retire and, indeed, after you lie down in bed. The Psalmist counsels us, "Let the godly exult in glory; let them sing for joy on their beds" (Psalm 149:4, ESV). Only recently, I have found this practice helpful in suppressing demonic dreams and interference with restful sleep.

Prayer, Fasting and Fellowship

Prayer is, of course, foundational to victory and specific content has already been discussed. But at certain crucial points early in the battle, my mother's prayers and laying on of her hands sustained me. I didn't learn until shortly before her death in 1999 that she also fasted secretly. I also did some fasting after I regained physical strength. And we received prayer support from the Christian community through local churches and the Christian radio station during the first few weeks while I was still in California.

Fellowship, too, was important, although I didn't share details of my affliction widely given the church's general ignorance of spiritual warfare then. Shortly after my return to the University the previous fall, I had begun attending a nearby Southern Baptist Church, the church I had casually visited the previous Easter before my return to faith. Providentially, the church had begun, not mere revival meetings, but a continuing spiritual revival based on the pastor's and then others' experience of the Lordship of Jesus Christ and practice of personal holiness. When I returned to school in January 1971, every week I attended all the regular church meetings plus one or more of the dozen or so spontaneously formed small group prayer meetings. Just being around serious, enthusiastic Christians and joining with them in praying and sharing was a great comfort.

For demonically occupied Christians lacking such extensive fellowship, my counsel is to be thankful for whatever church fellowship God has given you and to press into it heartily. While it is desirable that someone on the pastoral staff understand your affliction as you do, don't make a precise understanding of this controverted condition a basis for continuing fellowship unless the church does. I attended one church at school and another during the summer, and none of the pastors at either church understood my demonization. Indeed, the pastor of one flatly denied that it was possible, but I benefited from attending both churches.

Put on the Full Armor of God

In battling against demon affliction, Paul's command in Ephesians 6:11-20 is to put on the full armor of God because our "wrestling" is not with flesh and blood, but with evil spiritual entities. The fourfold emphasis of verses 11-14 on *standing* against these demonic powers implies perseverance in opposition to them. I didn't realize it, but once the covert spiritual warfare turned overt and I knew whom I was fighting, my victory was certain in Christ—as long as I stood my ground and resisted Satan, that is, as long as I didn't give up. Unfortunately, American culture today fosters, instead of perseverance under suffering, self-indulgence: That way lies dishonor, defeat and death.

The Magisterial Reformers Luther and Calvin were acutely aware of their continuing battle against Satan and his demons. In his *Institutes of the Christian Religion*, Calvin writes:

> We have been forewarned that an enemy relentlessly threatens us, an enemy who is the very embodiment of rash boldness, of military prowess, of crafty wiles, of

untiring zeal and haste, of every conceivable weapon and of skill in the science of warfare. We must, then, bend our every effort to this goal: that we should not let ourselves be overwhelmed by carelessness or faintheartedness, but on the contrary, with courage rekindled stand our ground in combat. *Since this military service ends only at death, let us urge ourselves to perseverance* (Book 1, Ch. XIV, §13, p. 173, emphasis added).

The means of resistance, then, include both the elements of the armor and prayer. The armor begins with the belt of truth, which is primarily the truth of the gospel of Christ that has set us free from sin (John 8:31-32) and secondarily the truth that we are sinners whose sins have subjected us to demonization. The breastplate of righteousness is primarily the righteousness of Christ that covers our sins and renders us invulnerable to Satan's accusations and secondarily, personal integrity. The readiness that comes from the gospel of peace is our God-given heart's inclination to share the truth of the gospel of Christ with other sinners so by all means follow your heart to share Christ in the midst of your affliction. The shield of faith is our trust in Christ that unites us with him and enables us to snuff out Satan's temptations before they enflame our passions and cause us to sin.

The helmet of salvation is the assurance of eternal life, of the final victory, that helps us persevere under the present sufferings of our affliction by the devil. The sword of the Spirit is the word of God used offensively to rebuke Satan and his lies and defensively to encourage ourselves in faith, in obedience and in our identity in Christ (e.g., Romans 8:14-17). Finally, petitions for ourselves and intercession for other Christians and especially for those advancing the gospel enable us both to defend ourselves and to join the offensive in advancing Christ's kingdom of light (Colossians 1:12-14). Applying these elements of gospel life assures us of our victory in Christ now and forever.

Physical Means of Resistance

I began a long-term habit of running and other exercises as a direct response to the physical weakness the spirits caused in my body. I also found that binding a cloth headband firmly around my head at night helped relieve headaches associated with my deliverance. And the high-pressure showers in my dormitory were also helpful. I certainly didn't attribute any ritual significance to taking showers, but they did seem to bring some relief.

Thus, I took up an across-the-board resistance to every demonic hindrance, physical or spiritual. Such holistic resistance accords with Paul's balanced view that "physical exercise has some value, but spiritual exercise is much more important" (1 Timothy 4:8a, NLT).

Sanctification: Victory over the Flesh

God has given ample provision for living a joyful Christian life graced by the fruit of the Spirit yet many Christians never experience this. But the way to victory over one's habitual sins such as lust and pride is open to those who take up their cross and accept the death to self that Christ pioneered for us on Calvary.

Thus, Paul writes in Romans 6:2 that we died to sin and continues in verses 6 to 7: "For we know that our old self was crucified so that the body of sin might be rendered powerless, that we should no longer be slaves to sin—because anyone who has died has been freed from sin." Get it? When Christ died 2000 years ago, we died because God already saw us "in Christ." So how do we experience this freedom from our enslaving sins? Again, in verse 11: "Count yourselves dead to sin but alive to God in Christ Jesus." So just believe God's word instead of our contrary experience. Look at it from God's eternal perspective instead of from our temporal one.

Thus, one night in Berkeley in 1974, the Holy Spirit showed me both that, in myself, I was helpless before my lust to masturbate and that, in Christ, I was dead to it. From 1970 until then, God had given me an inexplicable freedom from my besetting lust, but then I lapsed back into it a few times. I was very distressed by these failures, but then surprised by the Spirit's dissolving that desire even as I was about to succumb to it again.

Another perspective on this experience of victory over sin is suggested by Ephesians.5:18-20: Here being filled with or controlled by the Holy Spirit is expressed in worship of the Lord Jesus Christ and thanksgiving to God the Father. The key is submission to Jesus Christ as Lord as required for salvation by

Romans 10:9 and as Christ's reason for dying and rising "that he might be the Lord of both the dead and the living" in Romans 14:9. Thus, a willed surrender to the lordship of Jesus Christ leads to being filled with the Spirit and victory over habitual sins.

Biographies of Christians such as Hudson Taylor tell of their discovery of the "exchanged life." Ron Dunn approaches this victorious life through biblical typology in his *Victory for Ordinary Christians*. (See bibliography, p.138.) But the life these men and women experienced is found first in Scripture, notably in Romans 6, Ephesians 5 and Colossians 1 to 3. So the discipline of reading, memorizing and meditating on the Scriptures under girds the work of the Spirit that overcomes the flesh and sets us free.

The paradox, then, is that, avoiding the previously rejected passivity, we still must rely on a power not our own, the "Christ in you." Then, when victory over the flesh is received, we must recall in humility that our new virtue is pure gift, God's grace.

The Indispensable Virtue: Perseverance

If you are a believer under severe, demonization who has recognized your bondage and want to throw it off, seemingly unbearable suffering may be your lot for a time. The devil will bedevil you in countless ways. That is his job and he is devilishly good at it. In your suffering, you may shed many tears, but don't forget to laugh at that proud spirit as day after day you see his empty threats to destroy you thwarted even in the midst of your agony of suffering and weakness. Rely fully on Christ's words in Hebrews 13:5 never, ever to leave, never, ever to forsake you. Know that in the original language his promise is enforced with a fivefold negative. Believe it and heed the many biblical counsels to rejoice in suffering and persevere in doing good:

But we also rejoice in our sufferings, because we know that suffering produces perseverance; perseverance, character; and character, hope. And hope does not disappoint us, because God has poured out his love into our hearts by the Holy Spirit, whom he has given us (Romans 5:4-5)

"Do not be deceived: God is not mocked, for whatever one sows, that will he also reap" (Galatians 6:7, ESV).

20

Bible Evidence that a Christian Can Have a Demon

During the Cold War against the Soviet Union, American Central Intelligence Agency (CIA) officer Aldrich Ames acted as a double agent for the Russian spy agency, the KGB, for 8 years. After inflicting irreparable damage on American intelligence by betraying U. S. spies in Russia, some to their deaths; Ames was discovered, prosecuted and sentenced to life in prison in 1994. He was well aware of the penalties he faced if caught because the U. S. Government always warns citizens entering security agencies of the severe penalties the law has if they betray their country and serve any other power. Nevertheless, Ames contacted enemy agents who paid him very well for his treason. And today, he is still serving his life sentence in a federal prison.

I believe that every member of the Church of Jesus Christ is more actively targeted for compromise by the invisible agents of our Adversary, the devil, than members of the CIA were targeted by the KGB. C. S. Lewis takes this view in his *Screwtape Letters* in which he portrays the demon correspondents, whose letters make up his book, as collaborating to compromise one Christian. And most churches with a vital faith in Christ do teach their members that Satan and his demons are real. But in contrast with this world's security agencies, many churches fail to warn their members of the severe spiritual consequences of yielding to demonic counterfeits.

Thus, Christians need to know that the sins that may cause Pagans to be occupied by demons will have the same effect on them. If anything, Christians who *unrepentantly* indulge in anger, bitterness, unforgiveness, witchcraft, occultism, drug use or fornication will be more consistently and more severely afflicted by demons than unbelievers because Christians are targeted by Satan as potential threats to his kingdom. In addition, Christians need to know that demons may approach them posing as a dead relative, as an angel of light or as one of the Persons of the Trinity. As I told in Chapter 15, I was deceived into bridal mysticism by a demon posing as Jesus.

Nevertheless, because the Scriptures nowhere directly state whether or not a Christian can have a demon, this question is still hotly debated. Therefore, we must consider both the relevant biblical principles and what the Scriptures do say about receiving demons into the body.

"Having a Demon" and "Demonization" Defined

"Having a demon" (from Greek *echôn,* "having," and *daimónion,* "demon") is the phrase most commonly used in the New Testament for a person's having a demon or evil spirit in the body and being under an influence ranging from limited to complete control. "Being demonized" (from Greek *daimonízomai*) is the second most commonly used term, and Alexander Souter defines it as being "under the power of an evil spirit or demon" (*A Pocket Lexicon to the Greek New Testament*, p. 58).

The Gerasene demoniac of Mark 5, with his many occupying spirits and their apparently complete control of his actions to the point of violent insanity, is the most extreme biblical example, and both of the cited terms are applied to him. But *daimonízomai* is also used for less severe cases and as a general designation for the many persons brought to Jesus out of whom he cast demons with a word (Matt. 4:24, 8:16; Mark 1:32). Thus, demonization is not defined in Scripture by the demons' particular manifestation or degree of control, but by their mere presence where they do not belong—within the human body. Thus, the most common biblical terms for demon affliction, "having a demon" and "being demonized," are equivalent. Therefore, any person having a demon or demons in his body is "demonized." And for Christians, the final goal of demons is always the same; for as Jesus put it, "The thief comes only to steal and kill and destroy" (John 10:10a).

The traditional English words for the condition of a person occupied and controlled by demons are "demon-possessed" (e.g., Mark 5:15-16, 18) and "demon possession." Even if these terms are not taken to imply ownership of the demonized person by demons, they do imply an either-or condition of demons in control ("possession") or demons not in control (only influencing or afflicting from without). But if the degree of control demons exercise over a person from within can gradually increase with time, then demonization is not an either-or condition in terms of control, and the affected person is not like a football "possessed" by the team on offense. Instead, the demonized person is more like a wrestler gripped by holds of different kinds representing increasing degrees of control until he is pinned to the mat if the demons gain complete control. This control can take either the form of the self-destructive and anti-social maniac of Mark 5 or of the contented cultist willingly serving his satanic master.

All Christians must wrestle with evil spirits and *there is* an either-or condition in this wrestling that is implied by the most common biblical designation of demonization, that of having a demon, i.e., having a demon in the body. Thus, to have a demon in the body is to be demonized whether its influence is noticed or not. Certainly, if the demon is within the body, it has gained a favorable position for controlling the person, but this vantage point is not sufficient for total control as shown by the Scriptures, which record many cases of demons being cast out although their control was less than that exhibited by the Gerasene demoniac.

Thus, the original Greek verbs in the New Testament denote only the person's occupation and control to some extent by demons. And of course, Satan and his demons do not ultimately possess, in the sense of owning, anything, certainly not a Christian who belongs peculiarly to God as his child. Therefore, I think it biblical to call persons occupied by demons, "demonized," leaving the degree of control open to observation. This term is similar to the grammatical form of the original Greek present and aorist participles of *daimonizomai* in Mark and the other gospels and avoids the misleading implications of "demon-possessed," whether of ownership or of a high degree of control.

In preparing this chapter, I consulted Gary Graff's analysis of all New Testament Greek terms on demonic affliction in Chapter 8 of his three-volume study, *Can a Christian Have an Unclean Spirit?* I have relied on his observations and agree with his thesis that a Christian can have a demon, but I did not adopt his restriction of *daimonizómenos* to demonic occupation with a high degree of control. Since the Scriptures do not clearly limit the term to severe cases, I take it to represent a continuum of demon control from unnoticed to total.

The Relevant Biblical Principles

The biblical principles that we reap what we sow and that God does not show favoritism contradict the idea that Christians can escape the same temporal consequences that Pagans face for their disobedience to God. Thus, few would suggest that Christians who habitually take drugs or have promiscuous sex will not face the *normal physical consequences* of their sins: drug addiction or sexually transmitted diseases. But if Pagans who habitually fornicate, take drugs or practice witchcraft receive demons as a result and Christians who do the same things don't; the biblical principle that "a man reaps what he sows" (Galatians 6:7b) would be violated. If Pagans suffer demonization for such things, Christians must suffer the same consequences for their actions—or else there is favoritism with God. But the Scripture says, "God does not show favoritism" (Romans 2:11).

No, God does not arbitrarily protect his disobedient children from the *normal spiritual consequences* of their actions, including demonization. Instead, he permits us to learn obedience through suffering both the physical and the spiritual consequences of our disobediences. Thus, Christians can be demonized if they persist in willful disobedience to God. This argument from biblical principles and the analogy of physical to spiritual consequences of disobedience is enough in itself to establish that a Christian can have a demon. But before pursuing further biblical evidence for this conclusion, consider the apparent strength and the fatal flaw of the main counterargument.

The Counterargument

Now some Fundamentalist and some Pentecostal groups deny that a Christian can ever have a demon in his body, much less, be controlled by one or more of them. This theological position makes it impossible for them to warn against the dangers of demonization. In addition, their skepticism makes it very difficult for them even to minister to demonized Christians who sense that somehow evil spirits have entered into their bodies.

And the logical argument these groups make against the possibility of a Christian's having a demon seems compelling at first glance: The Presence of God excludes the presence of Satan and his demons as light excludes darkness; the body of the Christian is the temple of God indwelled by the Holy Spirit; therefore, a Christian can never be occupied or controlled from within by demons. But this formally valid syllogism is fallacious because the major premise that the Presence of God excludes the presence of Satan is unbiblical.

First, Satan's continued existence since his fall shows that omnipresent God constantly tolerates—more, sustains—Satan in His Presence. And the Book of Job twice shows God talking with Satan in the very throne room of Heaven (Job 1:6-12; 2:1-6). Of course, these biblical examples do not prove that a Christian can have a demon, but they do demolish the *a priori* argument to the contrary by showing that its major premise—that God and Satan cannot coexist in the same place—is false.

The Direct Biblical Evidence

Consider how 1 Timothy 4:1-2 suggests the possibility of spiritual seduction as well as doctrinal deviation when Paul writes, "But the Spirit saith expressly, that in later times some shall fall away from the faith, giving heed to seducing spirits and doctrines of demons" (ASV). The distinction of the "seducing spirits" ("deceiving," NAS, NIV) from their "doctrines" may be significant. In my experience of demonization as a Christian, the seducing spirits themselves were able to stimulate my senses and emotions and to inject deceiving thoughts directly into my mind without using any false prophets to speak false doctrines to me.

Where do false prophets like Edgar Cayce and Joseph Smith get their revelations and false doctrines anyway? According to their testimony, they had intercourse with spirits they believed to be of God. As a Christian, I was also able to have intercourse with evil spirits claiming to be Jesus. Although I was deceived about their identity and received these spirits into my body, God used my persistent reading and heeding of the Bible to keep me from being further deceived by any of the false doctrines that they could well have used to mislead me into a cult.

The Apostle Paul may speak directly to this issue of whether or not a Christian can have a demon in the body as follows:

> But I am afraid that as the serpent deceived Eve by his cunning, your thoughts will be led astray from a sincere and pure devotion to Christ. For if someone comes and proclaims another Jesus than the one we proclaimed, or if you *receive* a different spirit from the one you *received*, or if you accept a different gospel from the one you accepted, you put up with it readily enough (2 Corinthians 11:3-4, ESV, emphasis added).

As in 1 Timothy 4, the deception has two basic elements: false doctrine and false spirits. The preaching of another "Jesus" and the acceptance of a "different gospel" are the aspects of false doctrine ("doctrines of demons"). But the warning in verse 4 of 2 Corinthians 11 not to "*receive* a different spirit from the one you *received*" seems to be a warning against receiving spirits other than the Holy Spirit, that is, evil spirits. Skeptics correctly observe that *lambáno* has a wide range of meaning and could merely imply demonic influence. Therefore, let us closely consider New Testament usage of this term in relation to *spirit* or *pneûma*

This Greek verb *receive* (*lambáno*) is the usual word used to describe receiving a spirit (*pneûma*). In addition to 2 Cor. 11:4, *receive* also appears in relation to *spirit* in John 7:39, 14:17; 20:22; Acts 8:15-19, 10:47, 19:2; Romans 8:15; Galatians 3:2; and 1 Cor. 2:12. And this last verse is remarkable for its ellipsis that uses only one occurrence of *receive* to indicate reception of both good and evil spirits: "We have not *received* the *spirit* of the world but the *Spirit* who is from God" (1 Cor. 2:12).

Together, the three previously listed verses from John further sharpen the definition of this crucial term, *receive/lambáno*. John

7:39 explains that the believers "were to *receive* . . . the Spirit" but that he "was not yet given, because Jesus was not yet glorified" (NAS). In John 14:17, Jesus calls the Holy Spirit "the Spirit of truth, whom the world cannot receive, because it does not . . . know Him, but you know Him because He abides *with you* and will be *in you*" (NAS). And in John 20:22, after he was glorified, Jesus "breathed on them, and said to them, *'Receive* the Holy Spirit'" NAS). These verses show that for "you," the disciples, to "receive" the Spirit meant that the Spirit moved from being "with you" to being "in you" (14:17). That "in you" means "in your body" is thus apparent and is further evidenced by Paul's assertion—in the context of sexual sin involving the body—"that your body is a temple of the Holy Spirit, who is *in you*" (1 Cor. 6:19) Thus, the normal New Testament meaning of *receive* in relation to *spirit* is *accept into the body*.

Moreover, in the crucial verse, 2 Cor. 11:4, *lambáno* is used both of reception of "a different spirit" (an evil spirit) and of reception of the Holy Spirit ("the one you received"). The verbs differ only in tense (present vs. aorist). Since the Holy Spirit is received into the believer's body, this parallelism strongly implies that the evil spirit is also received into the body. Thus, if 2 Cor. 11:4 uses *lambáno* in the same way it is used in relation to *spirit* elsewhere in the New Testament and in the first part of this verse in the same way it is used in the last part, this verse is a warning to Christians against receiving evil spirits into their bodies. Since the Bible nowhere denies this possibility, it is the part of wisdom to seriously consider the arguments that a Christian can have a demon made by Evangelical scholars, missionaries and teachers such as the late Dr. Merrill F. Unger, Dr. C. Fred Dickason, Dr. Keith M. Bailey and Dr. Ed Murphy. Indeed, I maintain that acknowledging that a Christian can have a demon or be demonized is the key to both prevention and treatment of demon incursion among Christians.

Limits of Demonization

No doubt the control demons can exercise over a Christian is ultimately limited by God. Nevertheless, credible missionaries and deliverance ministers testify that demons can suppress a Christian's mind and express their evil personalities through him in speech and action to the point of demonization commonly called "possession." My demons were never able to control my speech and actions, but I was subjected to the devastating physical harassment and mental anguish described in Chapters 14 to 17. I had demons, and plenty of them, in my body; and they caused my muscles to twitch, caused my heart to skip beats and jerked my limbs and jaw. Their presence weakened my muscles, hindered my thinking and *did control* my emotions, filling me with fear and anxiety. Their intent, I believe, was to suppress my mind and control my body with the goal of my suicide since I was not open to the false doctrines they probably had hoped to promote through me. After they had suddenly turned against me, I eventually realized that I had been deceived and occupied by demons. Only then did I begin to consistently resist them and seek counsel on how to do it.

Demonization: Gradual Process, Stepped Series, Abrupt Onset or Combinations of These

In the Old Testament, King Saul experienced the abrupt onset of transient demonization as a judgment of God when, for his disobedience, "the Spirit of the LORD departed from Saul, and an evil spirit from the LORD tormented him" (1 Samuel 16:14, ESV). But since the Scriptures do not detail how demonization occurs in most cases, this must be determined from the experiences of Christian counselors and survivors of demonization. Thus, I became demonized gradually and unconsciously over many years through masturbation and associated experiences of passivity. Then, I began to receive the spirits consciously through my acceptance of false mystical experiences. Finally, I experienced an abrupt onset of emotional and physical affliction by the demons received previously. So my experience breaks down into 1) a gradual process over 20 years, 2) a stepped series of entrances of individual demons over 6 months, and, finally, 3) an abrupt attempt to suppress my mind and take control of my body. From this I conclude that demonization can develop either through a combination of these elements or by any one separately.

Therefore, demonization may be a completely gradual process of which the victim remains ignorant even as he becomes the willing tool of alien intelligences as he is seduced by demons into a cult. This is the deceived state of the neatly dressed cultist who knocks on your door. (Fear him not; instead show him compassion by sharing with him your testimony of God's grace.) But demonization can also be a stepped series in which the victim consciously receives different spirits at different times as I did and as do the devotees of some Pagan religions. Then, too, it can be an abrupt takeover of the human person by demons as a result of a specific sin that may (or may not) entail transference of spirits from a guru or occultic practitioner. Finally, demonization might proceed through an unholy combination of any two or all three of these demonic devices.

Thus, demonization is not a natural process working itself out through impersonal laws. Instead, demonization is the result of the interactions of intelligent personal beings, human persons and evil spirits. The chief weapon of Satan in this contest is the lie, deception. The battleground is primarily the mind of the Christian but can also become the body if the Christian gives "place" to the devil. The Christian's defense depends on accurate knowledge of the truth, which is why the subject of this chapter is so crucial— and so hotly contested among Christians.

Hope for the Demonized: The Truth

Christians, then, are constant targets of demonic intelligence agents who seek to disable them spiritually by any means possible. Unless they repent, Christians who are spiritually seduced into the sins that cause demonization in Pagans will surely be demonized and rendered useless as combatants in the spiritual battle raging everywhere on planet earth. And God will not arbitrarily prevent this normal spiritual consequence of his children's disobedience because that would violate the unchanging principles of his not showing favoritism and of your reaping what you sow: "Do not be deceived. God cannot be mocked. A man reaps what he sows" (Gal. 6:7).

The premise that God and Satan cannot occupy the same place is disproved by the contrary biblical examples cited, thus refuting the argument based on this premise that demons and the Holy Spirit cannot simultaneously dwell in a Christian's body. As we have seen from 2 Cor. 11:4, the Scripture warns Christians against receiving a spirit other than the Holy Spirit they have already received. And if the Bible warns Christians against receiving a different spirit, the danger of such reception must be taken seriously.

The truth that a Christian can, indeed, have a demon should not be distressing to obedient Christians who avoid both the obvious sins of anger, fornication, occultism and drug use (biblical *pharmakeía*) as well as the habitual practice of the less obvious sins of gossip, lying, greed and unforgiveness. All these invite the entrance of demons by giving place to the devil (Ephesians 4:26-27). The Christian who has unrepentantly practiced such sin to the point of demon occupation will probably need some help from the body of Christ to overcome both his sins and the evil spirits that reinforce his bondage to them. Recognition of his abnormal—but not uncommon—condition, instead of denial of its possibility, is the first step to learning the humility and obedience that lead to liberation.

But Christians such as I was, who have been seduced by spirits pretending to be a person of the Trinity, are likely to experience great confusion before realizing that they have been occupied by demons. The sin to be confessed is idolatry, which, once recognized, is readily renounced with spontaneous revulsion.

In the next and final chapter, I tell why understanding that a Christian can have a demon or be demonized is vitally important whenever revival breaks out.

"It is good for me that I was afflicted, that I might learn your statutes" (Psalm 119:71, ESV).
"Revive us and we will call on your name" (Psalm 80:18b).

21

Afterword and
A Caution for the Coming Revival

Consequences: Suffering

Over 40 years have passed since I was seduced by a demon posing as Jesus shortly after my return to fellowship with Christ in 1970. As with those who have violated their allegiance to their country with worldly secret agents, the consequences for me have been severe. Contrary to my expectation of rapid if not immediate deliverance—but in accord with the old Pastor's counsel—my deliverance has been gradual, not to say glacial. It took about 6 months to get over the worst of the emotional turmoil and mental confusion the spirits provoked in me. My ability to concentrate and study was hindered somewhat for a year or more, but by means of prayer and Bible reading, I kept my mind clear enough to maintain a respectable place in my graduate program for the additional year and a half I remained in it.

I Still Await Total Deliverance

For a long time I occasionally had difficulty distinguishing between feelings of devotion to the Lord and a sensuous imitation to which I was vulnerable because some of the evil spirits remained. And indeed, I have yet to receive complete deliverance from all of the many evil spirits I so willingly received. Recurring symptoms include unrestful sleep and demonic nightmares such as

I have had on some nights after working on this book. A less common symptom is muscular twitching. But I rarely have to deal with panic attacks anymore since I finally learned to rejoice in them as a chance to humiliate my enemy by exercise of Christ's authority. It is to laugh, indeed, when they and their fears must give way to your rebuke in Jesus' name.

On the other hand, during all my waking hours, I still have a curious pressure in my mouth that forces small bubbles of saliva out between my lips when I purse them. This started only some time after I began to oppose the evil spirits within, and I originally thought it to be caused by the evil spirits slowly leaving my body. But demons usually exit rapidly, even explosively, and the continuation of this phenomenon for so many years makes me uncertain of whether it is a result of their leaving or just an evidence of their residual presence. This is something that I have not heard of elsewhere. I disclose it as being appropriate to the genre of the confession and for the benefit of Christian theologians studying demonology. Despite my practical success in wrestling with my demons, I still don't have all the answers.

Because the Lord did not choose to remove all of the evil spirits I received through my sinful conduct and because sexual intercourse readily transmits demons from person to person, it might not have been appropriate for me to marry. So I received the unexpected gift of singleness along with the virtue of self-control. This gift of singleness has its compensations as the Apostle Paul points out in 1 Corinthians 7. Moreover, I have no immediate family to whom my confessions might be an unwelcome source of embarrassment. Therefore, I am content with my lot.

Why Deliverance May Be Delayed

Because of their unbroken record of success in driving out hundreds of demons with little delay, some savvy contemporary deliverance ministers may consider my incomplete deliverance unnecessary, even scandalous. But the Scriptures provide an instructive example with a possible explanation for my unusual condition. Like some of today's spiritual warriors, Jesus' disciples had enjoyed unbroken success in quickly driving out hundreds of demons from many people—until that fateful day at the foot of the Mount of Transfiguration when suddenly they found themselves unable to drive a demon out of a demon-afflicted boy. When they asked Jesus, "Why?" he replied, "This kind cannot be driven out by anything but prayer" (Mark 9:29, ESV). This need for prayer shows that—with a certain kind of demon—immediate deliverance isn't possible because prayer requires time. This also establishes the principle that deliverance may sometimes be delayed, depending on how God sovereignly responds to the prayers offered. This *kind* of resistant demon must be pretty rare, but its existence and our dependence on prayer to our Sovereign for its expulsion may explain delays in deliverance such as mine.

Nevertheless, rapid deliverance is to be expected in most cases. And one should beware of demonic lies that the sufferings they inflict are from God and must be stoically borne for his glory. Resist such lies with the many Scriptures that affirm the Lord's lovingkindness and with Psalm 34:19: "Many are the afflictions of the righteous, but the LORD delivers him out of them all" (ESV).

Consequences: Benefits

Insight into Demonization

When demons leave people completely controlled by them, the victims commonly have no memory of what happened while under demon control. Therefore, deliverance ministers who have dealt with many such cases may still be quite ignorant of what has gone on inside the demonized person. My conscious experience of the demons' focus on suppressing my brain suggests that they gain total control of their victims' bodies by, in effect, anesthetizing their victims by suppressing brain function. This would explain the inability of the severely demonized to recall events during periods of demon control.

Confidence to Share Christ with Cultists

Despite the slow pace of my deliverance, within 3 years I was writing articles exposing the concealed Hindu basis of Transcendental Meditation for publishers ranging from *Christianity Today* to InterVarsity Press. And I know that my demonization has made me less susceptible to oppression by the evil spirits of the false religions and cults I have studied. This is an important benefit for a writer investigating false religions. For example, some years ago I had an impromptu audience with

Tibetan Buddhist leader, Sogyal Rinpoche (author of *The Tibetan Book of Living and Dying*) in Weaverville, California, not far from the Chagdud Gonpa Monastery at Junction City that sponsored his appearance. During our friendly meeting, I shared the gospel with him; and I believe that he tried to impart some spiritual presence to me. But my experience of the demonic had prepared me to enter such an arena of spiritual warfare and emerge with a quiet joy at having had the privilege of confessing Jesus to a fellow sinner. Please pray for him.

Proposals for the Church Militant

Churches Should Regularly Use Their Authority over Demons

Even before Pagans poured into the church after Emperor Constantine professed Christian faith, the church realized that it needed to cast out the evil spirits most Pagans had received through their idolatry. Thus, the apologist Justin Martyr in his defense of Christianity to the Roman Senate in 150 A. D. cited the success of Christians in casting demons out of demonized Romans as an evidence of the truth of the faith (op.cit., Graff, v. 2, p. 173). More recently, during the Jesus Movement of the 1970s, front-line ministries to the Hippies routinely cast the demons out of their converts because most of them had been demonized through their sexual promiscuity, their nearly universal drug use and their frequent practice of Hinduism, Buddhism or New-Age religions.

In the conclusion to *Can a Christian Have a Demon?* Gary Hal Graff writes, "The power to free people from unclean spirits is resident within the church in one form or another [i.e., either by prayer or by command]; why not use it?" (v.3, p. 226). Why not, indeed! In view of the pervasive re-Paganization of American culture, I would suggest that churches consider a return to the ancient and salutary practice of privately commanding the demons to depart from new converts at their conversion and, again, at their baptism. In addition, the convert should renounce Satan and all his works and ways including, privately, their besetting sins because they may have caused demonization.

Certainly, whenever either long-time Christians or new converts have drug or sexual addictions or perversions, the demons from these practices should be ordered out in the name of Jesus *whether or not they choose to manifest their presence*. Moreover, ministry to adulterers, to lesbians, to homosexual men and to those confused about sexual identity should include the use of spiritual authority against the associated demons.

In Romans 1:26-27, the Apostle Paul points out that both lesbians and homosexual men have been given over by God to shameful desires and the resulting unnatural sexual acts. The NIV translates his characterization of these acts as "perversion" (ESV, "error") because of the abandonment of "natural relations" with the opposite sex. Demons are attracted by the perverse. Therefore, demonization is to be expected wherever there is sexual perversion, and it likely will be necessary to cast the demons out when such captives desire to be free. Repentant adulterers should also be encouraged to rebuke any evil spirits of adultery given place by their perverse violation of their marriage vows and of their one-flesh relationship with their mates.

Churches Should Reconnect Baptism and Communion

A while ago I visited an Evangelical church, where I witnessed the baptism of a woman who testified that she had received Jesus as Savior as a young girl many years earlier. Since she was now about to get married, she thought it was about time she got baptized. But who told her that? Many Evangelical churches don't even require an attender to be baptized before receiving communion. Could she have been reading her Bible on her own?

Indeed, some pastors tell unbelievers to receive communion as a means to receive Christ as Savior. But why encourage unbelievers who, according to the Scriptures, are spiritually blind to receive communion as an affirmation of a faith that they have not yet professed? If they have not been convicted of sin by the Holy Spirit, they may believe that such a mere act will save them, thus obscuring the truth that salvation is by grace through faith, not through any work.

Evangelicals in America need to recover the ancient understanding of baptism as the door of entry into the fellowship of the church and its importance as an integral part of salvation. The responsibility for laxity in obedience to Christ's command that those who receive the good news be baptized in the name of the Triune God lies primarily with the churches who fail to teach and practice prompt baptism of their converts. And the means to encourage prompt baptism are ready to hand: 1) Teach converts the necessity of obedience to Christ's command, and 2) Return to the traditional practice of requiring water baptism before admitting converts to the fellowship of communion.

A Caution for the Coming Revival

So there have been significant insights and evangelistic benefits from my sufferings. But the greatest such blessing may yet be the opportunity that publication of *Confessions of a Demonized Christian* has given me to warn the Body of Christ of a poorly understood aspect of the spiritual warfare going on every day on planet earth. My burden is especially for Christians who are earnestly seeking God as I was when I was deceived. Evil spirits particularly target such Christians for deception by approaching them as angels of light or as one of the persons of the Trinity. Enthusiastic Christians are Satan's prime targets for these deceptions because 1) such Christians are a threat to his kingdom, and 2) their seeking deeper experiences of God can make them vulnerable to spiritual counterfeits.

Now, when revival breaks forth once again in America as it did so unexpectedly in the late 1960s and early 1970s, this warning against the dangers of Satanic counterfeits of God's presence could help prevent any new revival from being derailed by the demon-inspired excesses that have bedeviled historic revivals such as the Welsh Revival of the early 1900s and the Jesus Movement of the 1970s. My prayer is that the Twenty-first Century church will be so well aware of demonic counterfeits that even in this evil day she will boldly take her stand against the devil's schemes to the glory of her Lord Jesus Christ.

The Last Word

I want to leave the last word of my story to the Holy Spirit who breathed out these words in the New Testament Scripture of the Epistle to the Romans:

> For I am convinced that neither life nor death, neither angels nor demons, neither the present nor the future, nor any powers, neither height nor depth, nor anything else in all creation, will be able to separate us from the love of God that is in Christ Jesus our Lord (8:38-39).

"Test all things; hold fast what is good"
(1 Thessalonians 5:21, NKJV).

Appendix A.
How to Avoid Demonization

Principles of Discernment

The Holy Spirit or the Evil Spirit?

Although the Bible applies the same word to describe receiving both the Holy Spirit and evil spirits because both take up residence in the body, the experiences are strikingly different. I received the Holy Spirit as did the Galatians (Ch. 3:2-4) by "hearing with faith" the message of Christ. This receiving was imperceptible to the senses but made me sensitive to my sins, grateful for God's forgiveness and sure that God was my Father. In addition, the Spirit set me free from my slavery to sin and gave me the power to overcome my besetting sins through my union with Christ in his death (Romans 6:1-14).

I first received evil spirits unconsciously and imperceptibly, but later I received them consciously in response to sensuous stimulation combined with their lie injected into my mind that this spiritual presence was "Jesus." Subsequent experiences of receiving the evil spirits into my body were physically palpable, and the results were sensual pleasure at first, but terror, confusion, despair, and fear of madness and death later when the demons turned against me.

Spiritual vs. Sensual

The contrasts between the way the Holy Spirit works and the way that evil spirits work make them distinguishable when their workings rise to the level of consciousness. Thus, although I know that the Holy Spirit indwells my body as his temple, I can't sense where he is. His operations within are fundamentally spiritual rather than sensate. The evil spirits, by contrast, made their presence felt in my skin, muscles, solar plexus and brain. Their physical and emotional effects seemed to have a neurophysiological rather than a purely spiritual basis. The main evidences of their presence within were stimulation of the senses (pleasant, painful) and emotions (pleasure, fear), of the muscles (trembling, twitching, jerking, weakness), of the skin (tingling, stinging or mildly burning sensations), of sexual sensations (pleasure) and of the head (pressure, pain).

Active Cooperation vs. Inactive Passivity

The Holy Spirit wants to enlist the obedient cooperation of the believer's mind, emotions, will and body in building up the body of Christ and extending God's kingdom (Romans 12:1-2, Ephesians 4:12-16). Christian submission requires the believer to actively apply his mind, his godly passion, his will and his body to his God-given tasks. The desired God-creature cooperation is described in Philippians 2:12-13: "Therefore, my dear friends, as you have always obeyed . . . *continue to work out your salvation* with fear and trembling, for it is *God who works in you to will and to act* according to his good purpose." God works in the believers' hearts, but they must diligently work out their salvation by willing and acting "according to his good purpose," that is, by *active cooperation.*

The evil spirit, by contrast, wants to impose his control over the believer's mind, emotions, will and body to hinder the growth of God's kingdom. To this end, the evil spirit works to render all of the believer's faculties passive, beginning with either the mind or the body since the two are directly connected. Therefore, whenever a believer expects to receive guidance by waiting passively on God with his mind unengaged and empty, he puts himself in great danger. The evil spirit will quickly take advantage of such a believer. His passive attitude leads readily to entry by demons and therefore must be avoided. *No prayer against the devil can prevent his working where a believer insists on being passive.*

Some Warning Signals

Some principles for discerning demonic activity follow. Take warning if you encounter any of these, and especially, as you seek God after submission to Jesus Christ as Lord and the resulting filling with the Holy Spirit. Those who break through the barrier of their besetting sins to victory over the flesh become a powerful threat to Satan's kingdom and may be tested by his diabolical counterfeits including even the charismas of the Holy Spirit. (See the discussion of spiritual counterfeits and other mystical deceptions under "Causes of Demonic Incursion" in Chapter 18.)

Demonic manifestations will cause unease and questioning in those sensitive to the Holy Spirit—at first. The first line of defense for a Christian, then, is the internal witness of the Holy Spirit. I beg you by the mercies of God not to disregard His gentle warning as I did. Thus, if you have doubts about the nature of a spirit, don't get into a conversation with him as I did—with disastrous results. The Bible says, "Resist the devil, and he will flee from you." Listen to the gentle voice of the Holy Spirit and rebuke the deceiving spirit in the name of Jesus. The demon likely will suggest to your mind that you are committing the unpardonable sin when you rebuke him. Don't believe this lie. You can't commit the unpardonable sin by mistake, and rejecting demonic lies is a major part of everyday spiritual warfare. It's all in the day's work.

Another warning of the presence of demons is fear. But familiarity with evil spirits can soon erase it. Nevertheless, an intuitive aversion to evil spirits from fear may give a demon away even when he poses as a dead loved one, an angel of light or a person of the Trinity. Don't ignore your fear, discern its cause.

Sensuous physical manifestations in the body such as a jerking of the limbs, a trembling of the flesh or a tingling, stinging or mildly burning sensation of the skin (pleasant or painful) are likely demonic. The Holy Spirit need not affect the body to accomplish his spiritual work whereas Satan typically works through the body and its senses to reinforce his lies injected into the minds of his victims. (These demonic phenomena call to mind the Mormon missionaries' heartfelt bearing of testimony to a burning in their bosoms as verification of the *Book of Mormon.*)

Any spiritual experience that puffs up its receiver with pride and renders him unteachable is questionable. I have met many people who have had dreams and visions of God and of Jesus. Unfortunately, their revelations typically contradicted the gospel of God's grace, and the persons telling of them did not live by biblical standards. They were usually so exalted by their unbiblical revelations as to be completely unteachable from the Scriptures. As

Paul writes, "Such a person goes into great detail about what he has seen and his unspiritual mind puffs him up with idle notions. He has lost connection with the head" (Colossians 2:18b-19a). Or as James puts it, "This is not the wisdom that comes down from above, but is earthly, unspiritual, demonic" (James 3:15, ESV). Christians sometimes may take undue pride in genuine spiritual gifts, but arrogance and unteachability suggest a demonic source for the experience giving rise to them.

Any physical or spiritual practice that renders the body or the mind passive is very dangerous because passivity is the necessary and sufficient condition for demon activity in human beings.

Three Questions for Discernment of False Spiritual Experiences

These five principles by which spiritual experiences may be tested are briefly summed up by the following three questions:

1. Does the practice or experience render my mind or body passive?

2. Did or does the spiritual experience raise any hesitation, question or fear in my heart?

3. Does the experience appeal to my senses, to my flesh or to my pride?

Test Spiritual Experiences

To avoid demonic incursion, then, Christians need to test all their spiritual experiences by the norms of Scripture. The foregoing principles and questions will help in such testing. This necessity should not be news to biblical Christians even if the danger of demonic incursion or demonization is. For John tells us in the context of a warning against false prophets, "Do not believe every spirit, but *test the spirits* to see whether they are from God" (1 John 4:1). And Paul says—in the context of the fire of the Holy Spirit and true prophecies—"*test everything*. Hold on to the good. Avoid every kind of evil" (1 Thessalonians 5:21-22, emphases added).

Because of an erroneous theology that says that a Christian's body cannot be penetrated by evil spirits, some groups encourage acceptance of any spiritual experience that comes to them as necessarily from God. But the previously noted apostolic warnings to "test the spirits" and to "test everything" show that this attitude is unbiblical. Paul's additional warning in 2 Cor. 11:4 against receiving a "different spirit" (ESV), shows the full danger of this undiscerning openness. Blanket acceptance of spirits without discernment of their natures is likely to lead to demonization.

No supernatural experience can be accepted as of God unless it is tested. I do not base this conclusion on my negative experience; it is just what the Bible literally says: "Test everything." And most spiritual manifestations and experiences must be tested and the genuine discerned from the counterfeit on the spot. If supernatural powers are manifested in meetings, spiritual discernment should be used to determine the source of the powers. If those leading such meetings are not exercising such discernment, the meetings, like some in Corinth, may do more harm than good. So whether in public meetings or private devotions, the individual Christian is always responsible to discern whether any spiritual manifestation is of God or of Satan. *No prayer against the devil can prevent his working in meetings where leaders and individual believers passively abdicate their biblical responsibility to test the spirits.*

Solitude, Silence and Rest vs. Eastern Spirituality

Is there no room, then, for solitude, silence and rest for the Christian warrior? Of course, there is. In Psalm 46, did not the *Lord of Armies* say, "Be still and know that I am God"? And when this very *Lord of Hosts* was on earth, he said to his disciples, "Come with me by yourselves to a quiet place and get some rest" (Mark 6:31b). Nevertheless, it is necessary to distinguish the Sabbath rest of Christ from the false rest of the meditative state of New-Age and Eastern spirituality. This altered state of consciousness is entered through the door of the blank-minded or passive state previously warned against as the necessary and sufficient condition for the working of demons in human beings.

The Key to Discernment of Misleading Meditative Practices: Repetitious or Uniform Stimulation of the Senses

The key to avoiding the meditative practices that lead to a passive state of mind is to grasp how the different techniques of Eastern meditation induce it. The basic model is the repetition of a mantra, which can be any syllable, word or phrase whatever. In Hinduism, for example, the mantra is often the name of a deity, but any word or phrase works just as well, whether, for example,

"Krishna" or "Jesus." Thus, the nominally Christian mystic who wrote *The Cloud of Unknowing* suggests meditating on a one-syllable word such as "love" or "God." And either silent repetition or shouted chanting of the words or phrases works similarly.

The continued repetition of any word or phrase readily shuts down the normal working of the mind through a psycho-physiological process akin to sense deprivation. This is the source of the "clear" or "centered" state of mind that leads, eventually, to the illusion of union with God in the unitive mystical experience. Since the "centering" effect of meditation is psycho-physiological, not divinely spiritual, it works the same without regard for the Pagan or Christian content of a mantra or chant. Again, by staring at a mandala or a candle, the sense of sight is similarly short circuited and the same mental state produced. *Any activity that causes either repetitious or uniform stimulation of a sense will have the same effect, e.g., the repeated gesture of the* mudra.

Nevertheless, by rendering the mind empty and passive, such practices do have the indirect spiritual effect of opening the body of the meditator to entry by demons. Therefore, maintain your normal mental state during prayer and genuine meditation on the word of God because 1) the engaged mind is the faculty through which God speaks to man and 2) the mind defends the body against the entry of alien spirits. If you would avoid demonization, then, avoid practices that render the mind disengaged, empty and passive ("clear" or "centered") as rigorously as you would avoid harboring the demons themselves.

Jesus' View of Eastern Meditation as a Way of Praying

Moreover, since mantramic meditation is understood to be a form of prayer in Pagan religions, consider Christ's words on prayer in Matthew 6: "And when you are praying, do not use meaningless repetition, as the Gentiles do, for they suppose that they will be heard for their many words" (v. 7, NAS). Since continued repetition of a word or of words quickly renders them opaque and meaningless to the mind of the reciter, Christ's words forbidding "meaningless repetition" apply directly to meditation on a mantra or even on the Scriptures when recited mantramically.

"If we confess our sins, he is faithful and just to forgive us our sins and to cleanse us from all unrighteousness"
(1 John 1:9, ESV).

Appendix B.
Childhood Masturbation

Sexual Conduct and Spiritual Warfare

Despite the scary example of my severe affliction by demons, partly through long-term masturbation, parents should not panic if they find that a child masturbates. It is only to be expected in fallen sons and daughters of Adam and Eve. But fear not! As Christians we have the solution for all sin: forgiveness *and cleansing* through Christ's death for *all* our sins. The difficult part is calmly and lovingly talking about sex with your child, but that is your responsibility as a parent.

To be sure, parents should not permit computer access to or possession of pornography and should also control access to movies and videos. But given the American advertising industry's addiction to the motto, "Sex sells," you may have to abandon television entirely. Sexually suggestive TV advertising has become so pervasive that children's innocence can hardly be preserved even until puberty if you have a TV set in the house.

Since sexual conduct is on the frontline of spiritual warfare, why not approach it as resistance to Satan's plan to alienate your children from God by temptations to enjoy sexual fantasies, masturbation, pornography and fornication? Children should be taught that the pleasures of sexual sin are the bait that demons use 1) to separate them from God, 2) to gain entrance to their bodies, 3) to misdirect their lives and even 4) to control them directly in greater or lesser degree through demonization, just as happened in my life.

Then, they can see that the battle to control their desires and say no to sexual sin becomes significant for both their temporal happiness and their eternal reward. Warn them that Satan wants to destroy them while Jesus wants them to enjoy fullness of life, usually in the lifelong covenant of marriage, which is a picture of the relationship between Christ and his church (John 10:10, Ephesians 5:25-32). So integrate spiritual warfare into conversations about sexual conduct and use our race's curiosity about spirits and demons to grip your child's attention and to teach them the spiritual facts of life: *Sexual sins give place to the devil as surely as unresolved anger, drugs and occultism do.*

Since tempting pictures, sexual fantasies and masturbation are entrance points for sexual sin, these should be discussed early on in conversations on sexuality. Self-control and purity should be portrayed as powerful virtues that fit one for service to God and for successful marriage. Fornication, adultery, sodomy *and masturbation,* on the other hand must be exposed as cheap and tawdry substitutes for the real fulfillment of soul-to-soul intimacy possible only in the God-ordained union of marriage. Ask for God's help and *calmly* show your child from the Scripture (Matt. 5:28) that sexual fantasies and masturbation commonly involve the sin of lust just like adultery. Teach them to confess such lust as sin and receive God's forgiveness in accord with 1 John 1:9, and, specifically, before receiving Communion.

The Spiritual Battle for the Mind

You should study together with them what the Scriptures say about our authority over demons from Luke 10:18-20 and Ephesians. 1:19-21 and 2:6. Then go on to teach them how to exercise that authority from James 4:6-8 and Matt. 4:4-11. Indeed, teach all your children how to rebuke demonic thoughts injected into their minds, as well as sexual and other temptations, by using the model of Jesus in the Temptation in Matthew 4. Have your children memorize verse 10 for this purpose, responding to demonic thoughts and temptations by speaking it into the atmosphere either in a normal voice or in a whisper. Shouting such a rebuke is neither wise nor necessary because its effectiveness is not a matter of power but of authority. If your child is not home schooled, you should teach your child the discretion not to speak this rebuke aloud where a teacher or pupil might hear it and cause problems.

If your child is born again (See Appendix C), admits to masturbating and wants to break the habit; establish accountability times. Study together Romans 6 and memorize together at least verses 1-11 and other verses on lust such as Colossians 3:5. Your child can personalize Romans 6:11 by affirming, especially when under temptation, "*I count myself dead to masturbation but alive to God in Christ Jesus.*" Study Romans 6 on the believer's victory over sin until it becomes real in experience for your child, when the Holy Spirit renews his mind through the power of God's word and his submission to the lordship of Jesus Christ.

If you have adopted children, you should calmly take spiritual authority over any spirits that might have gained entrance through heritage or abuse and command them to depart. Similarly, if there are indications of demonization in your natural children, you must not only pray for them, but also use the authority of the name of Jesus on their behalf until they have been born again and have been taught how to defend themselves spiritually with the sword of the Spirit and the authority of the name of Jesus.

Poltergeists and Masturbation

If your children tell you about strange noises in their bedrooms not explicable by natural causes, the noises may be made by poltergeists or noise making spirits. Their presence is not an indication of demonization, but does suggest sinful activity such as masturbation, and their noise making could be an invitation to communicate with them. So if poltergeists seem to be the cause of the noises, tell your children about them and their connection with masturbation (Ch. 6, "Masturbation and Poltergeists"). Then, casually ask if they have masturbated. If they deny it and you are not sure whether or not they are lying (as may happen with this sensitive subject), just go ahead and use the occasion for training and instruction in the Lord (Ephesians 6:4) *on this subject of spiritual warfare and masturbation.*

Consider any invading poltergeists as just so many spirit lab rats: Use them to show your children how to wield the believer's authority over Satan. In the presence of your children, calmly order these demons out of your house in the name of Jesus. Then, tell your children to let you know if the noises return. If they come back, inform the kids that sins like séances or masturbation invite the spirits right back in and ask whether they have done anything that might have invited the spirits back. Pray for your children and for wisdom and discernment for yourself in this battle.

Love Conquers Anger

Love your children by teaching them what they need to know about sex and spiritual warfare. Whatever your children do, avoid scare tactics and anger towards them because these are counterproductive. The Scriptures warn fathers in particular against the anger that provokes anger and rebellion in children. Thus, in Ephesians 6:4, the Apostle counsels: "Fathers, do not provoke your children to anger, but bring them up in the discipline and instruction of the Lord" (ESV). *After all, have you, yourself, never been guilty of sexual sin in thought, word, deed or desire?*

"'If anyone would come after me, let him deny himself and take up his cross and follow me. For whoever would save his life will lose it, but whoever loses his life for my sake will find it'"
(Matt. 16: 24-25, ESV).

Appendix C.
Childhood Professions of Faith

Discerning Spiritual Life

God has given to parents the primary *ministry* of reconciling their children to God. According to the Scriptures, children who have not yet trusted Jesus for salvation are spiritually dead in Adam's inherited sin. But Christ has graciously done everything necessary for their salvation, and the Holy Spirit is ready to apply this work to them. Parents, then, can lead their little ones to Christ by daily prayer for them, by being living examples of Christ's life and by lovingly sharing the word of God with them from birth. But it is the Spirit who must birth them from above by the imperishable seed, "the living and abiding word of God" (1 Peter 1:23).

Parents can determine whether or not the child who wants to be baptized (or confirmed) is trusting in Christ alone for salvation by asking the gospel-outline questions. These questions from D. James Kennedy's *Evangelism Explosion* help the parent and the child see what he or she is trusting in for salvation. I like the way Bill Fay uses these and two other question in his Radio Bible Class booklet, *How to Share Your Faith Without an Argument.* His first question helps discern whether the person has *a personal relationship* with God: "Who is Jesus Christ to you?" A merely theological answer such as, "The Son of God," is ambiguous. A relational answer such as "My Lord" or "My Savior" suggests that the person may have a personal relationship with Christ.

To test this claim, the next question is, "If, God forbid, you were to die today, where would you go?" If the child says, "To Heaven," the parent asks, "Why?" If the child's answer suggests they are depending to any extent on their good works, they are mistaken and probably are not saved. If the answer is ambiguous, restate the question in terms of this role playing situation: "If you were to die today and find yourself standing at the gates of Heaven, and if God were to say to you, 'Why should I let you into my Heaven to enjoy eternal life with me?' what would you say?"

If these questions show that your son or daughter is trusting in works instead of in Christ alone for entry into heaven, you can gently share the gospel again from the Scripture and wait for the Spirit of God to bring conviction of sin leading to repentance and faith. Parents should also see whether their children confess Christ as Lord in deed as well as in word before they are baptized.

In personal evangelism, I have emphasized the issue of the sinner's submission to Christ's authority as of the essence because of the condition of Romans 10:9 that you confess, "Jesus is Lord." To this end, parents should challenge their children with the words of Christ from Matthew 16:24-26. They need to realize that to be saved they must surrender control of their lives to the one who died for them.

Romans 10:12b-13 expands on this relationship when it says that the Lord bestows his riches "on all who call on him. For 'everyone who calls on the name of the Lord will be saved.'" I now encourage those who confess Jesus as Lord before me as a witness to call on the name of the Lord by also praying audibly to Jesus. The traditional sinner's prayer can be a way of calling on the name of the Lord. If a person is unable to pray aloud, his confession of Christ's lordship may be in some way deficient.

But using these powerful questions wisely requires discernment. This can be gained by using the questions to open up conversations about Christ with everyone you know, especially with fellow church members (who may not know the Lord). Then, when it comes to your own kids, you will know from experience how to deal with both sinners' evasions and saints' variations.

When your child shows clear evidence of knowing Christ, of having been born from above by the Spirit of God; he or she will want to obey Christ's command and be baptized. The holy and mandatory ordinance of baptism should then be administered by your church without delay.

"There are two equal and opposite errors into which our race can fall about the devils. One is to disbelieve in their existence. The other is to believe, and to feel an excessive and unhealthy interest in them"—C. S. Lewis.

Annotated Bibliography

Alexander, Brooks. *Witchcraft Goes Mainstream: Uncovering Its Alarming Impact on You and Your* Family. Eugene, OR: Harvest House Publishers, 2004, 284 p. Alexander prepares Christians to intelligently share the gospel with the Neopagan next door. He aims at understanding Neopagans and their influence on American culture, not at deliverance from demons. Online: www.apologeticsindex.org/2610-witchcraft-goes-mainstream-by-brooks-alexander.

Anderson, Neil, T. *The Bondage Breaker*. Eugene, OR: Harvest House Publishers, 1990, 249 p. Anderson emphasizes the liberating power of the truth of the Christian's identity in Christ.

Bailey, Keith M. *Strange Gods: Responding to the Rise of Spirit Worship in America*. Camp Hill, PA: Christian Publications, 1998, 242 p. This missionary to Native Americans warns of the need for deliverance ministry to the animistic peoples from all over the world now living among us, including Christians.

Basham, Don W. *A Manual for Spiritual Warfare*. Greensburg, PA: Manna Books, 1974, 157 p. I told Don of my incomplete deliverance in the late 70s; he was not perturbed by it.

Bubeck, Mark I. T*he Adversary: The Christian Versus Demon Activity*. Chicago: Moody Press, 1975, 160 p. Bubeck advocates both aggressive prayer and bold confrontation of evil spirits on the basis of the believer's authority in Christ.

Bubeck, Mark I. *Overcoming the Adversary: Warfare Praying Against Demon Activity*. Chicago: Moody Press, 1984, 139 p. Bubeck includes prayers of victory, for the filling with the Spirit, for taking up the full armor of God, etc.

Calvin, John. *Institutes of the Christian Religion*, ed John T. McNeill, tr. Ford Lewis Battles, Volume XX, *The Library of Christian Classics*. Philadelphia: The Westminster Press, 1960, hardback, 849 p.

Craig, William Lane. *Reasonable Faith: Christian Truth and Apologetics*, Wheaton, IL: Crossway Books, rev. ed., 1994, 350 p. Craig gives philosophical arguments for the truth of Christianity developed in his graduate course in apologetics.

Dickason, C. Fred. *Demon Possession & the Christian: A New Perspective*. Westchester, IL: Good News Publishers, 1989, 355 p. This scholarly approach to the Scriptures and to Christian experience shows that Christians can be demonized and gives practical advice to counselors and to the demonized.

Dunn, Ronald. *Victory for Ordinary Christians: Lessons in Living from the Book of Joshua*. Ft. Washington, PA: CLC Publications, 2011, ©1976 by Ronald Dunn, 109 p. Ron was my pastor at the church I attended in Texas, and I recommend his book to any reader seeking victory over sin and Satan.

Excel, G. W. "Do You Know How to Resist Satan?" Sized and formatted like a Campus Crusade booklet, this black-covered booklet taught how to recognize and rebuke Satanic thoughts injected into the mind. Although no longer available, I honor Brother Excel for his reproducible concept that was a life-saver for me. My booklet listed below is designed to fill this gap in the literature on resisting the devil.

Fay, Bill. *How Can I Share My Faith Without an Argument?* Grand Rapids, MI: RBC Ministries (www.rbc.org), booklet, 32 p. Fay's approach enables the witnesser to gain permission to share the gospel from the Scriptures and to avoid "bruising the fruit" if a person is not ready to hear the gospel.

Graff, Gary Hal. *Can a Christian Have an Unclean Spirit? Volume I, Satan and the Angels*. El Cajon, CA: Christian Services Network, 2002, 199 p. Graff says that his purpose is not only to prove that Christians can have demons, but also to encourage the church to exercise its power to cast them out.

_____. *Can a Christian Have an Unclean Spirit? Volume II, The Psychology and Book Apologetics*. El Cajon, CA: Christian Services Network, 1999, 249 p.

_____. *Can a Christian Have an Unclean Spirit? Volume III, The Theology and History*. El Cajon, CA: Christian Services Network, 2001, 232 p.

Haddon, David A. *Beat the Devil: Basic Tactics of Spiritual Warfare*. Redding, CA: Self-published booklet, 1992, 16 p. This booklet tells how to detect satanically injected thoughts and how to use Scripture and the authority of the name of Jesus against them following the example of Jesus in the temptation. This authority springs from your relationship with God through faith in Christ and your submission to Jesus as Lord.

Lewis, C. S. *Mere Christianity.* New York: Macmillan Publishing Co., Inc. 1943, 1945, 1952, 1960, 190 p. A standard defense of the Christian Faith.

_____. *Perelandra.* New York: Macmillan Publishing Co., Inc., 1944, 222 p. The battle with demons for control of one's mind is well portrayed in this book in protagonist Ransom's friend's encounter with a mental barrage early in the book and in Ransom's rebuke of the enemy spirit near its end.

_____. *The Screwtape Letters with Screwtape Proposes a Toast.* San Francisco: HarperCollins Publishers, 1942, 1996, 209 p.

Montgomery, John Warwick. *Principalities and Powers: A New Look at the World of the Occult.* Minneapolis: Bethany Fellowship, 1973, rev. 1975, 255 p. This Lutheran theologian presents his scholarly perspective on demonology, the occult.

Murphy, Edward F. *The Handbook for Spiritual Warfare.* Nashville: Thomas Nelson Publishers, 1992, hardback, 593 p. This is a thorough, biblical handbook on spiritual warfare.

Murray, Andrew. *The Power of the Blood of Jesus.* Ft. Washington, PA: CLC, 1963, 96 p. Victory is in the blood.

Nee, Watchman. *The Spiritual Man.* In Three Volumes, 1968, reprinted as a combined edition, 1977, New York: Christian Fellowship Publishers, Volume 3, 231 p. Nee sees the mind as the focus of spiritual warfare and exposes how demons dull and control the minds of believers. I don't recommend vv. 1 and 2.

Penn-Lewis, Jessie, with Evan Roberts. *War on the Saints.* New York: Thomas E. Lowe, 1988, Ninth Edition, unabridged, 325 p. If you have been deceived by a demonic counterfeit, you can probably find your experience described in detail here. Less expensive but still useful abridged editions are available.

Russell, Jeffrey B. and Alexander, Brooks. *A History of Witchcraft: Sorcerers, Heretics, & Pagans.* London: Thames & Hudson. 2d ed., 2007, 216 p. Russell's book has been a standard history of European witchcraft. Alexander adds his knowledge of contemporary witchcraft to this second edition.

Souter, Alexander. *A Pocket Lexicon to the Greek New Testament.* London: Oxford University Press, 1916, reprinted 1966, hardback, 290 p.

Sproul, R. C. *Not a Chance: The Myth of Chance in Modern Science and Cosmology.* Grand Rapids: Baker Books, 1994, 256 p. Philosopher-theologian-communicator Sproul guts the materialist argument for self-creation and with clarity affirms God as the logically and ontologically necessary Being.

Strobel, Lee. *The Case for Faith: A Journalist Investigates the Toughest Objections to Christianity.* Grand Rapids: Zondervan, 2000, 409 p. Strobel interviews a noted skeptic and a series of defenders of the faith about common objections to it.

Tozer, A. W. *I Talk Back to the Devil*, ed. Gerald B. Smith. Harrisburg, PA: Christian Publications, Inc., 1972, 144 p. Tozer exposes Satan's scheme to keep believers in bondage to the fear of man and encourages us to submit to Jesus as Lord and defy Satan verbally, especially by expressing our joy in the Holy Spirit in praise and by witnessing to others.

Unger, Merrill F. *What Demons Can Do to Saints.* Chicago: Moody Press, 1991 (1977), 222 p. The late Dallas Theological Seminary Professor gives reasons for his change from denying that Christians can have demons to affirming that they can.

White, James R. *The Forgotten Trinity: Recovering the Heart of Christian Belief.* Minneapolis: Bethany House Publishers, 1998, 224. Only the full Trinitarian Faith overcomes Satan.

White, James R. and Niell, Jeffrey D. *The Same Sex Controversy: Defending and Clarifying the Bible's Message About Homosexuality.* Minneapolis: Bethany House Publishers, 2002, 254 p. Chapter 6 discusses Paul's view of the unnatural affections of lesbians and homosexual men from Romans 1.

White, Thomas B. *The Believer's Guide to Spiritual Warfare.* Ann Arbor: Servant Publications, 1990 (revised and re-issued, April 2011), 173 p. Chapter 6 lists natural afflictions resembling demonization and Chapter 7 discusses spiritual discernment.

www.ingramcontent.com/pod-product-compliance
Lightning Source LLC
Chambersburg PA
CBHW061732020426
42331CB00006B/1203